Helena Gomm

in company 3.0

PRE-INTERMEDIATE TEACHER'S BOOK

B1

MACMILLAN

Macmillan Education
4 Crinan Street
London N1 9XW
A division of Macmillan Publishers Limited
Companies and representatives throughout the world

ISBN 978-0-230-45514-6

This edition published 2014
First edition published 2003

Design by emc design Limited
Page make-up by MPS Limited
Cover design by emc design Limited

The publishers would like to thank the following people, schools
and institutions for their help in developing this third edition: Pat
Pledger, Pledger Business English Training, Hamburg; Louise Bulloch,
Intercom Language Services, Hamburg; Elbie Picker and David
Virta, Hamburg; William Fern, KERN AG IKL Business Language
Training & Co. KG, Frankfurt; Belén del Valle, ELOQUIA, Frankfurt;
Katrin Wolf, Carl Duisberg Centren, Cologne; Andrina Rout, Fokus
Sprachen und Seminare, Stuttgart; Gerdi Serrer, ILIC, Paris; Sylvia
Renaudon, Transfer, Paris; John Fayssoux; Kathryn Booth-Aïdah,
Araxi Formations Langues, Paris; Fiona Delaney and Allison Dupuis,
Formalangues, Paris; Francesca Pallot and Susan Stevenson, Anglesey
Language Services, Chatou, France; Paul Bellchambers, Business
and Technical Languages (BTL), Paris; Louise Raven, marcus evans
Linguarama, Stratford-upon-Avon.

Many thanks also to all the teachers around the world who took the
time to complete our *In Company* online questionnaire and who have
contributed to the development of the *In Company* series.

The author and publisher would like to thank the following for
permission to reproduce the following material.

Extract from 'Inside: travel survey results', published on
www.4hoteliers.com 26.10.2007, copyright © 4Hoteliers 2003.
Reprinted by permission of 4Hoteliers.com – The Global Hotel
& Travel News Portal. Quotation from Bob Burg. Reprinted by
permission of the author. Adapted material from the article 'The
10 Most Stressful Jobs of 2013', taken from www.careercast.com,
copyright © 2013 Adicio Inc. Reprinted by permission of Adicio Inc.
Adapted material from 'Imagining the Internet "The 2008 Survey"', a
project of the Elon University School of Communications and the Pew
Internet and American Life Project. All rights reserved. Reprinted
by permission of Elon University. Adapted material from 'How to
Avoid the Middle Seat', taken from www.etravelgear.com, copyright ©
1998-2010 iGear Stores/eTravelerGear. All rights reserved. Reprinted
by permission of the publisher. Material from 'Facebook Bought
Instagram to Bolster Its App Internet Ecosystem', contributed by
George Colony, published on http://blogs.forrester.com 10.04.12,
copyright © 2016 Forrester Research Inc. and/or its subsidiaries. All
rights reserved. Reprinted by permission of the publisher. Material
from 'Work related stress – together we can tackle it', published on
www.hse.gov.uk/stress by the Health and Safety Executive. Contains
public sector information licensed under the Open Government
Licence v3.0. Extract from 'The Future of Ecommerce' by Ilya Pozin,
published on www.about.com, copyright © 2016 About, Inc. All
rights reserved. Reprinted by permission of the author. Material from
the article 'The Importance of Telephone Communication in Business'
by Mary Nestor-Harper, copyright © 2013 Hearst Communications,
Inc. Reprinted by permission of the author. Material from the
article 'Telecommuting becoming more prevalent', first published
on the Mashable.com website 11.03.12. Reprinted by permission
of Wrightsmedia.com. Extract from 'Work-life balance debates
"over-simplistic"' by Judith Doyle, taken from www.personneltoday.
com 22.11.00, copyright © Reed Business Information 2013.
Reprinted by permission of Reed Business Information. Extracts
from 'Telecommuting has Mostly Positive Consequences for
Employees and Employers, Say Researchers', taken from http://
www.apa.org/news/press/releases/2007/11/telecommuting.aspx
19.11.07, copyright © 2016 American Psychological Association.
Reprinted by permission of the publisher. Extract from 'Time
Management for Small Businesses: Cut to the Chase' by Stefan
Töpfer, taken from www.sme-blog.com, copyright © 2007 Stefan
Töpfer, Chief Education Officer and Chairman of WinWeb. Reprinted
by permission of the author. Material from 'Leaders wanted…good
managers need not apply' by Annelize van Rensburg, taken from
www.talent-africa.co.za, copyright © Talent Africa 2013. Reprinted
by permission of the author. Extract from '8 Reasons You Aren't
Getting Things Done', published on www.timemanagementninja.com
13.01.12, copyright © 2016 Time Management Ninja. Reprinted by
permission of the publisher. Extract from 'Hiring and Firing' by Lou
Carloni, The Industrial Physicist, Vol.9, Issue 3, page 28, copyright
© 2003 American Institute of Physics. Reprinted by permission of
the publisher. Material from 'World's record breaking hotels' first
published in The Daily Telegraph (Australia) 22.08.09, copyright ©
2009 The Daily Telegraph (Australia). Reprinted by permission of the
publisher. Adapted material from 'Wasting Time at Work' by Galen
Black, published on www.vgg.com 02.05.01, copyright © 2001 The
Van Gogh-Goghs. Reprinted by permission of the publisher. Material
from 'British men are working the longest hours in Europe' by Paul
Sellers 18.01.13, copyright © 2013 Trades Union Congress. All rights
reserved. Reprinted by permission of TouUChstone blog: A public
policy blog from the TUC, http://touchstoneblog.org.uk/2013/01/
british-men-are-working-the-longest-hours-in-europe/. Material
from 'Yo, Yotel arrives at Gatwick' by Susan d'Arcy, first appeared
in The Sunday Times 24.06.07, copyright © Times Newspapers Ltd
2015. Reprinted by permission of Yotel Ltd.

Printed and bound by CPI Group (UK) Ltd, Croydon

2018 2017
10 9 8 7 6 5 4 3

Contents

Student's Book contents

Introduction

Spring has arrived, judging by the number of tourists that have appeared in the streets. Phil has an hour free before his next lesson. Picking out a nice café, he chooses a window table and orders a coffee. After spending a few minutes people-watching, he starts to think about the lesson he's just come out of: his first class with a new group of students at the central offices of a pharmaceutical company. Half the lesson was spent in an informal chat based on the needs analysis, and there seem to be some potential problems. Phil opens his briefcase and takes out his notes.

> Jean Claude Duval, Purchasing Manager. Pre-int. Has been studying English for 'many years'. Uses English at work most days in emails and phone calls to suppliers, though these tend to follow the same pattern most of the time also has occasional face-to-face meetings: wants to improve general communication for these has difficulty just chatting during breaks in meetings or over lunch.
>
> Anton Brun, IT Systems Manager. Int. Did three years' English at school. Doesn't currently use English at work, but thinks it will be 'useful for the future'. Mainly interested in social English. Fairly fluent, but some grammar problems.
>
> Marie Nöelle Rousillon, Chief Financial Officer. Pre-int. Studied English at school and university, but didn't use it for years. Has now had to start using English regularly in monthly meetings with the new American shareholders and feels 'completely lost'. And it isn't just the meetings – says she goes to hide in her office during breaks to avoid having to engage in any conversation. Also receives occasional phone calls, mainly to check financial information, but her bilingual secretary deals with emails.

Phil knows the company well. There's no way he can move Anton to another group at a higher level: the other classes are all in the research labs outside the city. And anyway, Anton's warmth and interest in people helped the group to gel and work more productively together. But will he get bored working at a lower level? As long as the topics are interesting enough, perhaps he'll stay focused. And Phil could give him extra grammar and vocabulary work, which he'd really benefit from.

Marie Nöelle's needs are certainly the most urgent, but also the most specialized, and will probably involve lexis the others have no need for. Still, terminology is probably not her main problem. The real challenge is coping with complex interactions. The skills she needs – getting her point of view across, understanding different opinions, dealing with telephone calls, handling social situations – are useful for just about everyone.

Jean Claude's most immediate need is probably to develop self-confidence. Lots of tasks with concrete outcomes, guided conversation on different topics and vocabulary building activities would suit him.

As he thinks things through, Phil begins to feel more confident. Now, what about writing skills?

in company 3.0

in company 3.0 is Macmillan's skills-based Business English series, aimed at professional, adult learners seeking to realize their full potential as speakers of English at work – both in and out of the office – and in social settings. This third edition builds on the success of the previous editions and has been enhanced and updated to reflect the realities of the 21st century professional. Business English learners now face a challenging, fast-paced, technologically-advanced workplace and the process of English language acquisition with in company 3.0 has been adapted to match this. In addition to a comprehensive Student's Book that offers quick and tangible results, the series now provides students with a wealth of new material online. This allows learners to extend their studies, not only within the classroom, but also outside of the traditional learning environment, on-the-move and in their own time.

Ten key observations regarding teaching English to professional learners underpin the in company series:

1 Professionals like to be regularly reminded why they are studying and what's in it for them.
2 They are used to goal-setting and time constraints, and tend to welcome a fairly fast pace.
3 They are motivated by topics which directly relate to their own personal experiences.
4 They expect to see an immediate, practical payoff of some kind at the end of each lesson.
5 It is English, not business, they have come to you for help with (but see 7).
6 They want to be able to actually do business with their English, rather than just talk about it.
7 They appreciate texts and tasks which reflect what they have to do in their job.
8 They also appreciate texts and tasks which allow them to escape what they have to do in their job.
9 They don't regard having fun as incompatible with 'serious learning' (but see 1 and 4).
10 They like to see an overall plan and method behind the classes they attend.

Practical approach

in company 3.0 Pre-intermediate is a practical course in how to do business in English. Recognizing that people need more than just phrase lists and useful language boxes to operate effectively in real-life business situations, each unit provides a substantial amount of guided skills work to give students the chance to fully assimilate the target language and 'make it their own', before going on to tackle fluency activities.

Target skills developed at this level include:

- describing your work and company
- using the telephone
- discussing pros and cons
- making comparisons
- networking
- writing emails and reports
- obtaining and giving information
- discussing change and developments
- dealing with social situations
- making requests
- discussing consequences
- making plans
- negotiating.

Having something to say

in **company** 3.0 Pre-intermediate taps into students' emotions, with the assumption that by focusing on areas which have some human interest or twist, students will have more to say. The classroom is an artificial environment in which imagination plays an essential role. It is unlikely that students will have to use their English in a situation in which they are approached by an executive headhunter (Unit 11, page 73) or discover that a job candidate is a fraud (Unit 14, page 89). Yet situations like these have a dramatic impact which makes the target language memorable.

Student's Book

in **company** 3.0 Pre-intermediate takes students through 20 progressively more challenging units which include describing your work and company, obtaining and sharing information, networking and travelling on business. The course reflects the need for students at this level to develop their grammatical competence, increase their lexical range and, above all, acquire strategies to communicate effectively in both professional and social situations.

Structure for the third edition

in **company** 3.0 Pre-intermediate is organized into five sections. Each section consists of three 'Business communication' units, a 'People skills' unit and a 'Workplace scenario'.

Business communication units

These units deal with business and communication skills through informative and interesting topics. These topics can be divided into four key areas of a business professional's life:

Work issues

These units are built around themes which are common to all working situations, such as work-related stress, time management, office gossip and working from home. The approach taken ensures that these topics are brought to life. For example, in Unit 14 Hiring and firing, the themes of sacking and labour conflicts have been included with the intention of generating strong opinion and interest in the classroom.

Travel

These units focus on the pros and cons of business travel, encouraging students to draw on their own personal experiences of doing business around the world. As well as reading interesting and discussion-provoking texts about international travel, students analyze the language of *doing* global business, in particular as regards negotiating and successfully making a deal.

Communication

Apart from touching on more traditional aspects of communication, particular importance has been given to the Internet and the role of information technology in present-day business practice. Not only does this reflect the reality of the IT revolution in the workplace over recent years, but it also gives students the opportunity to look at the conventions and language of this area, which are increasingly important in day-to-day business. Unit 19, for example, discusses the growing trend of e-work and the implications this has on our working lives.

Company life

These units include a focus on the different grammatical tenses to enable learners to discuss their routines, past experiences, achievements and future plans in relation to their work and their company. Students are also encouraged to think outside the realms of their own experience and use their imagination, for example, by inventing their own ethical start-up company (Unit 1, page 10) or writing a report on a company with problems (Unit 10, page 67).

📹 Every third Business communication unit concludes with a video: *In company interviews*. These interviews showcase real business professionals discussing the preceding unit topics, and give a context for students' own discussion and additional worksheet activities.

People skills

Acquiring communication strategies for a variety of work-related and social contexts and developing interpersonal skills is the main emphasis of these units. The functional language required for interaction with others is presented and practised through dialogues and extensive listening practice. There is some lexical input, but no grammar focus.

Workplace scenarios

A new feature of the third edition of in **company** are the five Workplace scenarios which provide learners with additional extended communication practice through a simulation of a real-life business situation. More importantly, these business situations are illustrated through video, providing students with a visual support to the Student's Book activities which allows them to develop a range of different skills, including perception of body language, comprehension of various accents and an understanding of the importance of interpersonal skills.

Each Workplace scenario uses video as a prompt for discussion and then as a model for the students' own free roleplay. This fluency activity is reinforced by a *Useful language* box, ensuring that students feel fully supported throughout their roleplay. A self-evaluation form for every roleplay also gives students the chance to assess not only their peers' performance, but also their own.

Vocabulary syllabus

in **company** 3.0 Pre-intermediate devotes a lot of attention to vocabulary, which is presented through both written and recorded texts. Students are encouraged to take note of common collocations and word-building, and this is reinforced by the vocabulary section of the *Language links* which follow each Business communication unit of the Student's Book. These exercises effectively double the lexical input in each unit and can either be set for homework or made the basis of vocabulary-building lessons.

Phrase banks

The *Language links* also include *Phrase banks*, which provide short summaries of the functional phrases covered in each Business communication unit. These can be used for reference and revision. In addition, each People skills unit includes a set of *Useful phrases* which highlights the key relevant language related to each specific skill.

The Workplace scenarios also provide *Useful phrases* to give learners additional support during their roleplays. These phrases are first heard in the videos and are then reinforced and extended in the students' own free speaking practice.

Grammar syllabus

At pre-intermediate level, although students have met some of the major grammatical structures previously, they are meeting others for the first time. The approach in in **company** 3.0 Pre-intermediate is to highlight the grammar as it naturally emerges in the activities. Meaning and concept are made clear through context and example, and provision is made for adequate controlled practice before students attempt to use the language in a more ambitious context. Throughout the course, there is a strong, progressive grammar syllabus, which learners particularly appreciate at this level. This is supported by 15 grammar sections within the *Language links* which follow each Business communication unit in the Student's Book. These provide more explicit explanations and practice exercises. An irregular verb list at the back of the Student's Book gives students an additional reference tool as part of their course book.

Controlled practice

For pre-intermediate students, the most appreciated parts of the lesson are often those moments when they are asked to produce stretches of accurate English in a controlled context. in **company** 3.0 Pre-intermediate places special emphasis on controlled practice as part of the build-up for fluency-based work. For example, students listen to a conversation and then reconstruct it from prompts before going on to act out their own dialogues. The Workplace scenarios epitomize this method of fluency practice. Students are provided with an audiovisual example of a dialogue, followed by controlled practice of a similar roleplay and then the chance to check this through further video input. Finally, they participate in their own, personalized roleplay.

in **company** Online

The addition of a blended learning element to the course gives in **company** 3.0 a neat and compact learning solution for both students and teachers. For students, this means the opportunity to practise their language online, via the Online Workbook, as well as on-the-move by downloading the class audio and video. For teachers, this online product means the ability to track students' progress through automatic gradebooks, the opportunity to download the audio and video content, as well as gain access to additional photocopiable material, tests and worksheets.

Online Workbook

The in **company** 3.0 Online Workbook provides extra skills, grammar and vocabulary practice for every unit of the Student's Book. It contains interactive activities, audio for listening practice and automatic marking – making it perfect for self-study. Your students can instantly check answers and try again, as many times as they want.

The Workbook is also linked to an online gradebook, which means you can see your students' marks for each activity as well as the progress they are making. Students will also be able to chart their own progress.

The Online Workbook contains 20 units to match the Student's Book. Students can read and listen to texts on topics similar to those featured in the Student's Book and develop the reading, listening and writing skills that each Student's Book unit introduces. Each Workbook unit also contains lots of extra grammar and vocabulary practice, and there is a grammar reference section for students to consult if they encounter any difficulties.

Resource Centres

In addition to the Online Workbook, students and teachers have access to the Student's and Teacher's Resource Centres. These contain a wealth of additional resource material for use both in and out of the classroom.

Class audio

This includes all audio tracks from the Student's Book class audio CD, along with full listening scripts. Students and teachers can download all the material to a mobile device for listening on-the-move.

Video 📹

In company in action videos accompany each Workplace scenario in the Student's Book. In the Teacher's Resource Centre, each of these videos has an additional classroom-based worksheet to fully exploit the audiovisual material, including teaching notes and answer keys.

In company interview videos showcase business professionals around the world discussing key business skills and topics. Each interview is supported by a self-study worksheet for students to complete at home.

All video material can be viewed online or downloaded to a mobile device for watching on-the-move.

Tests

Progress and placement tests allow teachers to assess their students' work throughout the course. The automatic gradebook on the Online Workbook also provides the teacher with instant feedback on their students' progress.

Additional student support

Students have access to the following resources to support their learning:

- Unit-by-unit glossary
- Student's Book answer key
- Student's Book phrase banks

Additional teacher support

In addition to the above, teachers have access to an additional 35 photocopiable worksheets which extend and/or revise elements of the Student's Book. The worksheets are written by ten practising Business English teachers and provide approximately 25 extra hours of material to supplement the Student's Book.

Fast-track map

An invaluable resource for the busy teacher is the new 'fast-track map' that accompanies every level of **in company** 3.0. This detailed map provides teachers with a fast-track route through the Student's Book, which is ideal for those students who have 30–60 hours of English lessons.

The fast-track map gives the teacher the option of following one of three routes (taster, language practice and language input), selecting the most relevant and useful activities to do in class. Each route also provides a comprehensive self-study plan, for students to enhance their learning outside the classroom.

Class audio CDs

Throughout the course, substantial use is made of audio recordings to input business expressions and grammatical structures. Indeed, very little of the language work is not either presented or recycled in a recording.

The recordings feature both native and non-native speaker accents, providing the students with extensive exposure to real spoken English. There is frequently an element of humour in the recordings which, besides entertaining the students, motivates them to listen again for things they may have missed the first time round.

There are full listening scripts at the back of the Student's Book. All Student's Book class audio material is also available online, accessible to both students and teachers through the resource centres. These audio tracks can be downloaded as MP3 files and played on various devices, from CD players to smartphones and tablets. This allows students to listen again to all audio material in their own time, even when on-the-move, giving them the flexibility to listen and re-listen to the class audio as much as they want.

In addition, the Listening section of the Online Workbook provides further listening practice with new recordings that students will not yet have heard in class.

How can I exploit the dialogues further?

Distinguish between different types of listening skills practice. The exercises are initially task-based activities which focus on comprehension. However, it is also important to give learners the opportunity to listen to texts again in a more detailed way. In other words, having understood what was said, you should then give some attention to *how* things are said. Try the following intensive listening techniques:

- Allow students to listen to the recording again in a relaxed way while they follow the listening script at the back of the Student's Book.
- Pause the recording after questions for students to recall or predict the response. (If they write these down as they go, you can ask them to recall all the questions at the end.)
- Pause the recording after responses to questions and ask students to think of other possible responses.
- Pause the recording in the middle of lexical chunks (collocations, fixed expression, set phrases) for students to complete them either orally or by writing them down.
- Ask students to write down a recording as you play it, line by line. If they miss a word, encourage them to look at the words around it and imagine what could go in the gap. Ask students to compare their transcripts to the original. Focus on common errors and spelling problems.
- Ask students to listen to a conversation and repeat it line by line. Then build up the conversation on the board using word prompts. Ask students to re-create the conversation from the prompts.
- Looking at the recording line by line, ask students to 'play' each line in their heads without actually speaking, and then listen and compare to how it actually sounds.

Reading texts

The reading texts in **in company** 3.0 Pre-intermediate have been chosen to involve, entertain and provoke students into lively discussion, as well as to contextualize key target vocabulary. Squeezing a text completely dry of all useful language usually demotivates a class, but many of the longer texts in **in company** 3.0 Pre-intermediate are information – and lexically-rich, and can usefully be revisited.

The reading section of the Online Workbook uses new reading texts, to provide further reading practice in a different context.

How can I exploit the texts further?

Try some of the following:

- Ask students to set each other questions on the text.
- Ask students to set you questions on the text, and vice versa.
- Give students several figures from the text and ask them to recall the context in which they were mentioned.
- Read the text aloud but slur certain words/ phrases and get students to ask you for repetition/ clarification.

- Give students the first half of between eight and ten collocations and a time limit in which to search for the collocates in the text.
- Give students a set of miscollocates and ask them to correct them by referring to the text.
- Read out the text, pausing in the middle of collocations / fixed expressions / idioms for students to predict the completions either by shouting out or writing down the answer.
- Read out the text, pausing at specific vocabulary items and ask questions like: *What's the opposite of X? What's the word we learned the other day which is like X? X is a noun: what's the verb form/adjective? X often goes with the word Y: what other words can go with Y? Give me another sentence using X.*
- Ask students to read the text aloud as a pronunciation exercise. Don't look at the text yourself as they read: this will force you to concentrate on the comprehensibility of their output. Ask them to do this in pairs.
- Write key words on the board relating to the main ideas in the text and ask students to reconstruct the text orally.

Fluency work

in company 3.0 Pre-intermediate includes two types of fluency activity which draw on both the specific language presented in a unit and the wider linguistic resources of the students. These are:

- roleplays and simulations, where students are given a scenario and perhaps some kind of 'personal agenda'
- 'framework' activities, where students decide on the content for an interview, report or phone call, and the Student's Book provides them with a linguistic framework to help deliver that information.

In order to avoid learner and teacher frustration, sufficient preparation for both types of activity is essential, and it may sometimes be advisable to carry out the actual fluency activity in a subsequent lesson to ensure plenty of time for preparation and feedback.

Working with video

Here are some suggestions of different ways of working with video.

Video dictogloss

This gives the students practice in grammar and vocabulary, with emphasis on sentence building. Use a short part of a video. Tell the students to watch and listen carefully as you play the extract. Play it once and ask them to write down in any order any words they can remember from the conversation. Then ask them to work first in pairs and then in small groups and to use the words they have written to recreate as much of the dialogue as possible. This activity works better with practice!

Questions for answers

This activity gives the students practice in prediction skills and practises question formation. Find five or six examples of questions and answers in the video script. Write the answers on the board or on a sheet of paper. Ask the students to work in pairs and guess what the questions for these answers are. Listen to their ideas, but don't correct them. Then play the recording so they can check if their predictions were correct.

Multi-listening tasks

This activity practises taking notes while viewing. Divide students into three or four groups, and give each group a different listening task. At the end of the viewing, groups exchange papers with someone else from the same group. Show the video again. Have them check their partner's answers and add more information. Finally, students form groups of three: with one person from A, B and C, and discuss what they learned.

Subtitles off/Subtitles on

This activity practises listening for detail. Write sentences from a section of the video, preferably a continuous conversation. Photocopy the sheet (one copy for every three students) and cut up the slips of paper. Put students into groups of three. Hand out a set of slips to each group, in the wrong order. As students listen to the video (subtitles off), they put the slips into order. Play the video again (subtitles on), so students can check their order. Finally, have them practise the dialogue in their groups.

Stop and predict

This activity motivates students and develops classroom discussion. Press 'Pause' at an appropriate moment and ask students to guess what is going to happen next. Alternatively, ask students what the speaker is going to say next. Elicit ideas from your class. Then watch the next part of the video and find out the answer. Who guessed correctly? This activity only works when students watch the video for the first time.

Shadow reading

This activity gives students practice in rhythm and intonation. After students have watched the video, give them a copy of a short section of the script, preferably a dialogue. Give them a few minutes to read it through silently. Get them to practise reading the text aloud in small groups. Then play the video again and ask students to read the script aloud in time with the video. This can be difficult for students at first but, with practice, it can really help with stress, weak forms and rhythm. Start by doing this with short sections and gradually increase their length.

Fast-forward viewing

This activity helps students to understand the main ideas. Write a few basic questions on the board relating to the video clip students are going to watch. Play the entire clip on fast-forward (no sound). Encourage students to guess the answers from the quick viewing. Elicit other details they learnt.

Teacher's Book

In this book, you'll find comprehensive teaching notes which give an overview of each unit, detailed procedural instructions for all the exercises and full listening scripts and answer keys.

A recurring feature of the previous edition is the inclusion of **1:1** teaching tips following every group-based or roleplay activity throughout the procedural notes. These have been updated and their number increased for this third edition. The aim of these notes is to offer tips on adapting the material to suit one-to-one classes, which are so common in in-company teaching. This allows the teacher to make better use of the material, in all teaching contexts.

The procedural notes also contain *Language link* highlights, which are reminders of exercises in the *Language link* pages where students can find grammar explanations or further practice in a particular grammar or vocabulary area. This allows the teacher to focus students' attention on particular areas of difficulty or interest.

We hope you enjoy working with **in company** 3.0.

Simon Clarke

September 2013 (with thanks to Mark Powell)

01 Introductions

Learning objectives

This unit is about introducing yourself, talking about your role in the company you work for, and describing companies and their main areas of operation.

Students begin by looking at some key vocabulary associated with different roles within a company and then listen to an extract from a communications training course in which the participants introduce themselves.

Next, students read a text about a professional networking site and look at one person's profile page. They discuss whether such sites can be useful for people in business.

In the next section, students listen to an extract from a radio programme and complete a company profile. They examine the use of the Present Simple for describing stable situations and the Present Continuous for describing current or changing situations. They also do some work on common collocations which are useful when talking about companies.

In the final section, students discuss ideas for a new start-up company. They then question each other about their new companies and write descriptions.

The grammatical focus in this unit is on the use of the Present Simple and the Present Continuous, and the lexical focus is on words for describing companies and roles within a business.

Digital resources: Unit 1

Online Workbook; Placement test; Extension worksheets; Glossary; Phrase bank; Student's Book answer key; Student's Book listening script; Fast-track map

The training course

In this first section, students begin by matching definitions to some useful words which they will encounter in this unit. They also listen to the start of the first session of a communications training course in which the participants introduce themselves to the group and talk about the companies they work for.

Warm-up

You might like to begin by finding out what type of company each student works for, particularly if this is a new class and students are unknown to you and to each other. If they all work for the same company, ask them to say what it is that they do for the company. If they are not yet employed, ask what kind of business they hope to get into.

Focus attention on the quotation at the top of the page and the question underneath. Explain or elicit the meaning of **networking** and ask the students to say how important they think it is in their industry or an industry they hope to work in.

 If you are teaching one-to-one, your first class is a good opportunity to find out what exactly your student's job entails, so that you have some idea of what topics are most likely to be of interest and the situations in which the student is most likely to have to use English.

1 Students do the matching individually at first and then compare their answers with a partner.

ANSWERS

a 1 b 4 c 7 d 2 e 3 f 10 g 6 h 9 i 5 j 8

2 Ask students to decide which of the words in 1 they associate with their own role at work.

3 **1.01** Ask students to listen to the recording and tick the words in 1 which they hear. You may need to pause the recording after each speaker or play it several times in order to allow them time to do this.

ANSWERS

d HR department   h management training
c retail chain   g sales and promotion
e campaign   a online services

1.01

A: Okay everybody, can we make a start? First of all, allow me to welcome you all to Ashbourne Management College. My name is Mariah Wilson and I am the main tutor for our 'Results Through Collaboration' course. It's always useful to know something about the background of the other participants so we normally begin by asking you to introduce yourself to the rest of the group. Perhaps we could start with you, Jan?

B: Yes, hello. My name is Jan Werner. I work for Metronet Fibre. Our main business is fibre optics. We install urban fibre-optic networks for telecommunication systems all over the world. I'm Director of Communications in the HR department. I'm Norwegian, but I live and work in the Czech Republic. Our headquarters are in Prague. That's where I'm based. At the moment, though, I'm spending a lot of time visiting our other offices in Europe. My job involves organizing and running different management training courses for our senior management.

A: Thank you, Jan. Silvia?

C: Well, I'm Silvia Fortuni. I'm Catalan and I'm from

Barcelona. I work for a big retail chain with franchises all over the world. We manufacture and sell clothes and fashion accessories, but my role is related to sales and promotion. I work out of our headquarters in Barcelona and I'm the Regional Director of Marketing there. I'm responsible for our campaigns in the European area. I have to say I love my job and I welcome the opportunity to learn something more about communication skills. I think that's it. If you want to know anything more, you can ask me.

D: My turn? Hi, everybody. My name is Jean-Christophe Marchal, but most people just call me JC. I'm Commercial Director at PPTT Services in Paris. We mainly work with big public companies in the Paris area. My background is in new technologies and I'm responsible for promoting and selling our ideas for online services and products. I'm in charge of quite a large team and good communication is essential. You probably think from my accent that I'm French. Actually, I'm Belgian but, I'm based in Paris, where we have our main office.

A: Thank you, JC. Now, Elena, I think it's your turn …

4 Focus attention on the chart and the photos of the people in the recording. Ask students to listen again and complete the chart. Again, pause or play the recording more than once to allow them time to do this.

ANSWERS

	From	Job	Home
Jan Werner	Norway	Director of Communications	Czech Republic (Prague)
Silvia Fortuni	Spain (Barcelona)	Regional Director of Marketing	Spain (Barcelona)
Jean-Christophe Marchal	Belgium	Commercial Director	France (Paris)

5 **1.01** Encourage students to try to complete as many of the sentences as they can before they listen again to check their answers.

ANSWERS

a name is; work for; main business
b I'm based
c is related
d out of
e responsible
f Commercial Director
g background
h in charge of

6 Tell students to work with a partner. First they should complete the table for themselves, and then they need to ask questions in order to complete the table for their partner.

 Ask your student questions first in order to demonstrate and note down their answers in the table. Then encourage him / her to ask you similar questions and to complete it for you. Then, either give a model introduction of the student first, or ask him / her to introduce you as if you were a speaker at a conference and follow this up with your introduction of the student.

7 Give students time to prepare their mini-presentations. Allow them to refer to their tables for help, but discourage

them from preparing and then simply reading out a description. Praise any use of phrases in 5.

 You could ask your student to prepare a mini-presentation introducing themselves for homework. This could be delivered in the next class. Be prepared to ask questions to elicit further information.

Language links

Direct students to the **Phrase bank** in the **Language links** section on page 11, which has a list of useful phrases for introducing yourself and talking about jobs and roles within a company.

8 Put students in groups and ask them to discuss training courses. As they work, go around giving encouragement and help with vocabulary. Encourage each group to report back to the class on the results of their discussion. If anyone has any amusing stories about training courses they have been on, encourage them to tell them to the class.

 This is a good opportunity to find out what experience your student has of training courses and to encourage him / her to talk about any courses he / she has been on. Be prepared to start off the conversation by sharing your own experiences.

Networking

In this section, students read a text about a popular online networking tool called *Work the Net*. They answer questions about it and then look at the *Work the Net* page for one of the speakers on the training course in the previous section. They discuss professional networking sites and how useful they are for people in business – and whether there are any problems with using them.

Warm-up

Introduce the expression *professional networking* and find out if students are familiar with professional networking sites like LinkedIn® and SkillPages, or social networking sites like Facebook and MySpace. Do not pre-empt the discussion at the end of this section, but quickly find out how many students use these sites.

1 Tell students to discuss the questions with a partner, before reading the text. Have a class feedback session, then ask students to read the text to check their answers.

ANSWERS

a Students' own answers
b It is a popular online networking tool that connects business professionals all over the world
c Professional people
d Information about companies and recruiters

2 Answer any questions students may have about the text and then ask them to find words and phrases in the text to match the definitions.

ANSWERS

a professionals b essential c database
d key contacts e being proactive

3 Focus attention on Jean-Christophe Marchal's *Work the Net* page and remind students that he was one of the speakers on the communications training course they listened to in the previous section. Go through the questions with the class and then ask them to look at the *Work the Net* page and find the answers.

ANSWERS

a Media industry and new TV technologies, social networks, TV on mobile, new technologies for flat screens, Microsoft Excel™, Microsoft Word™, PowerPoint, Microsoft Outlook™, SAP, Photoshop, Acrobat.
b Yes, he does.
c Yes, he is.
d PPTT Services
e He lives in Paris at 7, Rue Richard-Lenoir.
f He enjoys cycling, reading and philosophy.

4 Put students in pairs. Tell them to take turns asking and answering the questions from 3. Make sure they change the pronouns each time. For example: *What are your competencies and skills?* **Do you** *have a degree?*

 If you are teaching one-to-one, tell your student to ask you the questions and then reverse roles and ask him / her to answer them.

5 Put students in groups and ask them to discuss the questions about networking sites (both professional and social). Encourage them to report back to the class on their discussions.

 If you are teaching one-to-one, discuss the questions with your student. If you have an entry on a professional or social networking site, you might like to show this to your student and share your experiences of using such sites.

Language links

Direct students to the *Language links* section on page 11, for more useful vocabulary on companies and the Internet.

Company profile

In this section, students listen to an extract from a radio programme and complete a company profile. They then study the use of the Present Simple and Present Continuous in descriptions. Finally, they complete sentences with useful business-related collocations.

Warm-up

Find out whether your students like smoothies or other fruit-based drinks. If they do, ask them what flavours they like best. Have any of them ever had an Innocent smoothie?

1 **1.02** Focus attention on the list of figures. Tell students they are going to listen to an extract from a radio programme in which these figures are used. Ask them to listen carefully and number the figures in the order they hear them. Then play the recording. You may need to play it more than once. Go through the answers with the class and make sure everyone is clear on the pronunciation of these figures.

ANSWERS

Correct order: 7, 3, 2, 5, 8, 6, 1, 4.

1.02

Hello, and welcome to *Business Talk*. This month we're looking at the role of ethics in business. According to Richard Reed, co-founder of Innocent Drinks, the company behind award-winning fruit-based smoothies, ethics are fundamental to the company's success. Innocent says that, as well as making money, the objective is always to leave things a little bit better than it finds them, an inspiring way to approach business.

So, how did the success that is Innocent all begin? Innocent was founded back in 1998 by Richard and two friends from Cambridge University. They decided to set up a business together and spent £500 on fruit to make smoothies to sell at a music festival. A sign above their stall said 'Should we give up our jobs to make these smoothies?' They asked people to put their empty bottles in one of two bins marked 'Yes' and 'No'. At the end of the festival the 'Yes' bin was full, so they went into work the next day and resigned.

At first, finding investment was a problem until an American businessman, Maurice Pinto, put up the £250,000 they needed to get started. With a fresh image and careful use of social media for promotion, Innocent soon became one of the fastest-growing companies in the UK and enjoyed a significant period of success. However, some of its fans were disappointed when, in April 2009, Coca-Cola® bought a small stake in the company for £30 million. There was further negative publicity when, a year later, the multinational increased its stake to 58% for about £60 million. Innocent now operates from its headquarters in London as a subsidiary of Coca-Cola.

Despite any issues they've had, Innocent continues to innovate and the product range now consists of vegetable pots and other healthy, natural products as well as smoothies, and the company is constantly working on new lines. Innocent sells to over 10,000 retailers in 13 European countries, and its market is constantly growing.

So what is it that makes Innocent an ethical company? Apart from only using packaging that can be recycled, it uses only 100% natural products and each year gives 10% of its profits to charities in the countries where its fruit comes from.

Innocent wasn't the first company to tap into the fruit drink market, but it was one of the first. It's always important to be different from the competition and, with Innocent, the combination of ethics and clever marketing is a recipe for success.

2 1.02 Focus attention on the company profile. Tell students they are going to listen again to the extract in which this company is described. Ask them to look through the profile to see what kind of information is missing and see if any of them can remember any information from the first time they listened. Then play the recording and ask them to complete the profile. You may need to pause the recording or play it more than once.

ANSWERS

a 98 b smoothies c 13 d subsidiary
e social media f London g 10%

3 1.02 Ask students to complete the sentences. Then play the recording again for them to check their answers. Check answers with the class by asking students to read out the completed sentences so that they hear the phrases in context. Ask them what they notice about the answers (they are a mixture of Present Simple and Present Continuous).

ANSWERS

a 're looking b operates c continues d is constantly working
e sells f is constantly growing g uses

4 Remind students that the phrases they completed in 3 were a mixture of Present Simple and Present Continuous. Working with a partner, ask students to look back at the completed sentences and decide how we use the two tenses. Check answers with the class.

ANSWERS

a b, c, e, g b a, d c f

Language links

Direct students to the *Language links* section on pages 11–12, for more information and practice on the Present Simple and Present Continuous.

5 Ask students to work individually to write their questions, but allow them to compare with a partner before checking answers with the class. Students may come up with valid questions which are different from those given below. Accept any that are grammatically correct and make sense.

SUGGESTED ANSWERS

a What is the company's name?
b What are its main products?
c How much does the company give to charity?
d Who does the company sell to?
e What is Innocent's recipe for success?

6 Ask students to work individually to form collocations and decide which sentence to put them in. To make this more interactive and to check the answers, you could ask one student to read out the sentence stem and another student to provide the missing collocation. You might like to follow this up by asking students to use the collocations in sentences of their own.

ANSWERS

a natural products b success story c social networks
d Negative publicity e detailed information f product range

7 Ask students to discuss with a partner whether they agree with the sentences in 6, and why or why not. Then have a class feedback session.

Your start-up

In this final section, students invent a new ethical start-up company and describe it to a partner. They then write descriptions of their partner's company.

1 Go through the instructions and the table with the class. Students work individually at first. Give them time to think of ideas for their new companies and go around offering help and encouragement as they complete the first column of the table. Then ask them to work with a partner and take turns asking and answering questions about their partner's start-up company. They should complete the second column of the table with this new information.

2 Encourage students to use the framework to structure their descriptions. Ask several students to read out their descriptions to the class.

 Ask your student to think of ideas for a new company for homework and to come to the next lesson prepared to talk about it. Either tell him / her to use the framework in 2 to write a description of his / her own new company, or prepare ideas for one yourself. Tell the student to ask you about it and then write a description based on the information you give.

Language links

ANSWERS

Vocabulary
Companies and the Internet
1 a promote b franchises c responsible d website
 e investment f headquarters g Internet h sales
 i network j employs k retail
Jobs
2 a executive b chairman c retired d position e title
 f manager g accountant h president i description

Grammar
Practice 1
a am doing (T)   b sell (H)
c do/are doing (O)   d is selling (T)
e works (H)   f is thinking (M)
g am living (T)   h gets (H)
i thinks (O)   j is getting (M)
k are working (C)   l lives (H)

Practice 2
a How does the company make money?
b Why is your business expanding?
c Where are they setting up a business?
d How much money are you looking for?
e What kind of business experience does he have?
f What is their unique selling point?
g How many people does your company employ?
h Who is the manager of the company?
i Who are they talking to about further investment?

02 Work–life balance

Learning objectives

This unit is mainly about combining working life with home life. It begins by looking at a range of statistics about working hours and the work–life balance, and presents the profile of a top female executive who successfully combines her career with her family life.

In the next section, students listen to two people discussing the demands of someone's new job. They then discuss the demands of their own job or that of someone they know.

The unit then goes on to examine how people can balance work and leisure, and ensure that they reduce the amount of stress in their lives.

The grammatical focus is on expressing frequency, and the lexical focus is on work and routines, and discussing ideas.

Digital resources: Unit 2

Online Workbook; Extension worksheets; Glossary; Phrase bank; Student's Book answer key; Student's Book listening script; Fast-track map

In this first section, students begin by completing some statistics in an article about work–life balance. They check their answers and then discuss the situation in their own country. They then read the profile of a woman who combines a successful executive career with family life. They answer questions about her life and talk about how typical they think it is. They then practise using frequency expressions to talk about how often they do things.

Warm-up

Focus attention on the quotation from Confucius and elicit the meaning (if you love your job, then what you do every day won't feel like work at all). Ask students how important they think it is that they enjoy the job they do, and whether they keep their work and home lives separate. Find out how many hours a week they work and whether these are all done in the office, or if they sometimes take work home.

1 Ask students to read the article extract quickly, ignoring the gaps, so that they get an idea of what it is about. Then ask them to try to complete the gaps with the numbers in the box. Reassure them that they are supposed to guess the answers here and that you don't expect them to know them already. Make sure they have completed all the gaps before going on to 2.

ANSWERS

a 2   b 3   c 48   d 1,625   e 76,700

2 Ask students to turn to page 130 to check their answers. Before they discuss the two questions, elicit their reactions to the statistics. Was there anything that surprised them?

3 Ask how many of your students have children. Ask them if the company they work for helps them to combine their careers with their family responsibilities. Go through the questions with students so that they know what information to look out for when they read the profile.

ANSWERS

a 5.30 am
b 8.50 am
c Never more than an hour
d Using the phone is nearly always quicker than using email
e Only occasionally

4 Ask students to discuss the questions with a partner, then have a class feedback session.

5 Focus attention on the underlined word in the profile (*often*). Explain that this is a word we can use to say how frequently something happens. Ask them to go through the profile and underline any other words and phrases that tell us how frequently something happens.

ANSWERS

often; usually; every day; normally; usually; sometimes; never; once a month; constantly; whenever possible; nearly always; hardly ever; most days; don't often; sometimes

6 Ask students to look back at the phrases they have underlined in the profile and decide which is the correct option in each sentence.

ANSWERS

a before   b after   c beginning or end

7 Ask students to work individually to add frequency expressions to the sentences to make them true for them. Remind them that they may have to change the verb form. As they do this, go around and make sure that they are positioning them correctly. Ask several students to read out their sentences.

Language links

Direct students to the *Language links* section on page 18, for more information on the position of frequency expressions, and a practice exercise to help students put these expressions in the right place.

8 Ask students to complete the first two columns in the chart with activities related to their own daily routines. Then tell them to ask their questions to a partner and complete the third column. Have a class feedback session to find out what questions were asked and what some of the replies were. Ask students if they were surprised by anything they have found out about their classmates.

When your student has completed the 'You' part of the chart, tell him / her to ask you questions to find out about your daily routine.

Ask your student to prepare a profile that describes his / her own daily routine, using Sally McDermott's profile as a model. You could set this for homework and go through it in the next class.

9 Ask students to use the information from 8 to produce a profile of their partner's routine. This could be written and presented to the class, though confident students may be able to do it just by using their notes. When all the routines have been presented, the class could vote on who has the best work–life balance.

 Encourage your student to use the information they found out about you in 8 to produce and present a profile of your daily routine.

What's in a new job?

In this section, students listen to a conversation between two people discussing someone's new job, and what it involves. They then use prompts to write questions from the conversation, and listen again to check their answers. Then they use similar questions to find out details about each other in an information-gap exercise. They finish by asking each other about their own working conditions.

Warm-up

Ask students what they think are the advantages and disadvantages of having a new job. If they are slow in coming up with ideas, start them off with a few of your own. For example, a new job may mean more money and more responsibility; you may have to work very hard at first in order to create a good impression; you may be last in line when it comes to choosing when to take your holidays, etc.

1 **1.03** Go through the questions with the class before you play the recording, so that students know what information to listen for. Tell students to cover up the page below the photo as they listen, so that they can see exercise 1 but not exercise 2, which gives part of the listening script.

> **1.03**
> A: Hi, Eddie. How are you?
> B: Oh, hello, Jennie. I'm fine. And you?
> A: Fine thanks. How's Fiona?
> B: Oh, she's okay. She's got a new job.
> A: Really? That's good.
> B: Well, yes, I suppose so, but I'm worried she's working too hard.
> A: Oh, dear. Does it involve long hours?
> B: Officially 40 hours, but she often works late. We don't see her at home much.
> A: What's she doing?
> B: It's the same company – you know, educational software – but she's regional marketing manager for Latin America now.
> A: Sounds impressive. What does it involve?

B: Quite a lot! Apart from being in charge of the sales reps she also works on new product development and the whole marketing strategy of the company.
A: Does it mean a lot of travelling?
B: It seems to. At least a couple of trips a month.
A: I see.
B: I don't mind that. It's the weekends that cause problems.
A: Does she have to work weekends?
B: Not every weekend, but we can never make plans.
A: Oh, dear. How much holiday does she get?
B: It's not bad. Three weeks a year. But that's a long way off.
A: You're being a bit negative. Does she enjoy it?
B: It's hard work, but I think she enjoys the challenge.
A: But you're not very happy.
B: I'm happy for her. The money's good and it's great for her career, but there is a downside.
A: Well, it's always difficult at the beginning. Anyway, give her my regards. Why don't we go for a drink sometime?
B: Okay, I will and yes, I'd like that.

ANSWERS

a He is probably her husband or partner. Clues to this lie in Eddie's words *We don't see her at home much* and *Not every weekend, but we can never make plans,* which suggest that they share a house and are used to spending their free time together.

b He is pleased for Fiona because she earns good money and it's a good move for her career, but he worries that she works too hard. He is upset that she often works late and sometimes has to work weekends, which means he doesn't see much of her and they can never make plans.

2 **1.03** Go through the example with the class, then focus attention on the other prompts and the corresponding answers. Ask students to complete the other questions. Then check answers and any vocabulary queries with the class.

> **Language links**
>
> Focus students' attention on the frequency expressions in the conversation, such as *often, a couple of trips a month, not every weekend, never, three weeks a year.* The *Language links* section on page 18 has more information about expressing frequency, and exercises to practise using frequency expressions. This will help them when they come to ask and answer questions about their own working conditions.

ANSWERS

a Does it involve long hours?
b What's she doing? (*or* What does she do?)
c What does it involve?
d Does it mean a lot of travelling?
e Does she have to work weekends?
f How much holiday does she get?
g Does she enjoy it?

3 Ask students to turn to the relevant pages and look at their charts. Point out that they should ask questions similar to the ones in 2 to find out the information to complete their charts, but that sometimes they won't be able to use exactly the same questions. Give them a few minutes to decide what questions they will need to ask. As students ask and answer their questions and fill in their charts, go around making sure that they are formulating their questions correctly. Give help where needed. When they have finished, students check answers by comparing charts. As an extra check, ask several students to say what questions they asked to elicit the information.

Direct students to exercise 1 in the *Language links* section on page 17 for more practice on talking about the responsibilities and requirements of various jobs.

 Take the role of either Student A or Student B and do the activity with your student, giving him / her the chance to answer your questions as well as ask his / her own.

4 With a new partner, students take turns to ask similar questions about their partner's job (or the job of someone they know). Go around making sure that they are asking and answering correctly. Give help with any extra vocabulary they may need.

 Do the exercise with your student and be prepared to answer questions about your own job or one of someone else that you know well.

Taking things easy

In this section, the focus changes slightly, moving away from a concentration on the workplace to ways of maintaining a good work–life balance by keeping healthy and alleviating the stress that work often induces. Students complete a questionnaire about stress and exercise, then read an article in which a professor presents a rather unusual view on the importance of relaxation. They then talk about their own attitudes to exercise and relaxation.

Warm-up

Find out how many of your students belong to a gym. Ask them why they go, how often they go and what they do when they are there. Find out what other types of exercise your students take.

1 Students complete the questionnaire, which is about attitudes and beliefs about exercise, with a partner. Encourage them to compare their answers with other pairs to see if there is any consensus.

2 The article presents the rather unconventional conclusions reached by a German scientist on the benefits of being lazy rather than energetic. Give students plenty of time to read the article and ask one of them to give a brief summary of the ideas in it. Elicit their reactions to the article and answer any questions they may have about vocabulary.

3 Students read the article again more carefully to find and underline the two expressions.

ANSWERS

lazing around, to take it easy

4 Give students time to devise their own titles, then have a class feedback session and write some on the board. Ask students to choose the title that they think fits the article best: either one of those given in the Student's Book, or one of their own suggestions. Ask them to justify their choices.

Direct students to exercise 2 in the *Language links* section on page 17, which uses the ideas from this article to practise the language of work and routines.

Exercise 3 on page 17 also uses ideas from this article to practise *do* as an auxiliary.

At this point students might also like to do exercise 4 on page 17, which practises phrasal verbs.

5 Put students in groups and ask them to discuss the questions. Appoint a secretary in each group to take notes and report back to the class at the end on what was said.

 Ask your student the questions. Be prepared to offer your own opinions and talk about your own lifestyle.

ANSWERS

Vocabulary

Work and routines

1 a get; off b full-time; work c work; overtime d takes; hour e check; emails f ratio; to g productive; day

2 a 1 b 5 c 6 d 2 e 7 f 4 g 3 h 8

Do as an auxiliary

3 a Do b do c don't d does e doesn't
  f doesn't g don't h don't i doesn't

Phrasal verbs

4 a switch off b work out   c give up   d picks [me] up
  e use up f goes through

Grammar

Practice 1

a I travel abroad four times a year.

b We always have a department meeting on Monday morning.

c He doesn't often go to Germany.

d The department manager usually leaves early on Friday.

e I never use the car because I can't drive.

f She always has lunch in the office canteen.

g They aren't often late for work.

h Microsoft® is always in the news.

i I change my mobile every year.

j Do you ever have office parties?

k How often do you go to the gym?

l Do you use your laptop much?

Practice 2

a How do you go to work?

b How much/often do you use the phone?

c What time / When do you get to work?

d Why does he do the housework?

e How often does he play squash?

f Who does she go to work with? / With whom does she go to work?

g How do you spend the morning?

h How many hours a week do you work?

i How long does it take you to read the newspaper?

j Why do you work so hard?

03 Telephone talk

Warm-up

Focus attention on the quotation. Ask students whether Mary Nestor-Harper believes that the telephone is still important in business or not, and why. Explain that the quotation suggests that others may feel that it is outdated and superseded by other forms of communication. Find out if students agree.

In this first section, the focus is on the pronunciation of numbers. Students practise writing down numbers that they hear. They then put some useful telephone phrases in order, then practise dictating telephone numbers with a partner.

Warm-up

Put a few numbers that are of significance in your life on the board, e.g. the number of children you have, the number of years you have been teaching, your telephone number, the numbers in your car registration, etc, but don't say what they represent. Ask students to read them out and guess what they are. They can then work with a partner to write down their own significant numbers, then ask and answer questions about what they represent. Circulate and monitor, giving help as necessary.

1 🔘 **1.04–1.08** Tell students that they are going to listen to five phone conversation extracts. They have to write down the phone number that they hear in each one. The first part of the first number has been done for them. As two of the numbers are given in 2, ask students to cover this part of the page before they listen. Play the recording and pause it after each conversation to allow students time to write down the number. You may need to play it more than once to allow them to do this. Check answers with the class, calling on several students to read their answers aloud.

Draw students' attention to the use of the word *double* when talking about two consecutive numbers which are the same. This is very common when giving phone numbers.

ANSWERS

a 0837 621 882 b 90 358 6759   c 0453 678234
d 0766 349 3782 e 090 238 6980

 1.04

A

A: Yes?
B: I'd like to speak to Derek LaMotte, please.
A: Who?
B: Derek LaMotte. Is that ILM?
A: What number did you want?
B: 0837 621 882.
A: No, I'm afraid you've got the wrong number.

 1.05

B

A: You have one message from 90 358 6759 at 18.30 on April 1st.
B: Hi, it's Dave here …

 1.06

C

A: This is the BetaGuide directory service. Donna speaking. Which city?
B: I'm calling from Portsmouth. Can you give me the number of Budget Car Rental, please?
A: Just one moment. I have three numbers.
B: Oh. I need to call them to report a breakdown.
A: Okay. It must be this one.
B: I think the number …
C: The number you require is 0453 678234. The number you require is 0453 678234.

 1.07

D

A: UKN Systems. Janet speaking.
B: Morning. My name's Peter Bland from Pressic SA. I arranged to meet Derek LaMotte at a factory out here on the Houghton Industrial Estate, but I can't find it. Could you give me his mobile number so I can ask him where it is?
A: Err, yes. Just one moment.
B: It's probably just around the corner.
A: It's 0766 349 3782.
B: I'm sorry. Could you say that again more slowly?
A: 0766 349 3782.
B: Right. Got it. Thanks.
A: Bye.
B: Yeah. Goodbye.

 1.08

E

Remember, you have the chance to win £1,000. Ring now on 090 238 6980. I'll repeat that for you. If you know the answer, phone us now on 090 238 6980.

2 **1.04–1.08** Tell students that they are going to hear the five conversation extracts again. This time, they have to number the phrases in the order in which they hear them. Go through the phrases with the class first so that they know what information to listen out for. Play the recording and check answers with the class.

ANSWERS

a 1   b 3   c 6   d 4   e 2   f 5

3 Students discuss the phrases with a partner and decide which ones they think will be useful for them to know. They then underline these. Ask several pairs to give their opinions.

4 With the same partner, students practise dictating telephone numbers to each other.

1:1 Prepare a list of numbers to dictate to your student. If possible, do this via a telephone call and ask the student to bring the list of numbers to your next class.

Language links

Direct students to the *Language links* section on page 24 for more practice on numbers and telephone phrases.

Polite questions

One way to avoid conflict on the phone is to sound polite and friendly. This section focuses on indirect questions as a way of sounding more polite.

1 **1.09** Before students complete the questions, elicit from one student an example of a direct question and then ask another to turn it into an indirect (polite) question. Establish that indirect questions make people sound more polite. Ask students to listen to the conversation and try to complete the questions with the actual words used. You may need to pause the recording and play it several times to allow them to do this. As they complete the questions, go around helping them with the construction of polite questions. Play the recording again for students to check their answers. Demonstrate how much gentler and more pleasant indirect questions sound, by saying first the direct question and then the polite equivalent.

ANSWERS

a Do you know what the flight number is?
b Could you tell me what time it gets in?
c Do you know if there's any delay?

1.09

A: InterAir, can I help you?
B: Yes, please. I'd like some information about a flight arriving from Munich.
A: Yes. Do you know what the flight number is?
B: The flight number? I'm not sure. I know it leaves Munich at 17.30.
A: Oh, yes, that's IA 345.

B: Yes, that's it. Could you tell me what time it gets in?
A: Yes, the arrival time is 19.10.
B: 19.10. Do you know if there's any delay?
A: No, the flight is on time.
B: Right, thank you very much.
A: You're welcome. Goodbye.

2 Direct students to the prompts on page 130. Students work with a partner to repeat the same conversation that they heard and read in 1, but without reading it straight off the page. The more you can get students' eyes off the page and looking at each other when they practise conversations, the better and more natural they will sound and the more fluent they will become. When students write their own conversations to practise in class, it is a good idea to encourage them to write prompts only, rather than the full text.

3 Focus attention on the correct word order in example sentence a). (There is more on word order in direct and polite questions in the grammar part of the *Language links* section on page 25.) Students rewrite direct sentences b) to k) in their polite forms, using the chart below as a guide. Check answers by having one student read out the direct question, sounding deliberately abrupt, and another reading out the polite question, sounding excessively polite. This is quite fun to do, and the more students exaggerate their intonation, the more likely they are to appreciate and remember the difference between the two types of question.

ANSWERS

a Could you tell me / Do you know what time the flight leaves?
b Could you tell me / Do you know which terminal it leaves from?
c Could you tell me / Do you know how far the factory is from the airport?
d Could you tell me / Do you know how long the meeting with Mr Fuentes is?
e Could you tell me / Do you know which car hire company it is?
f Could you tell me / Do you know which models they have available?
g Could you tell me / Do you know if I need an international driving licence?
h Could you tell me / Do you know where we are staying?
i Could you tell me / Do you know if it is a nice place?
j Could you tell me / Do you know how far the hotel is from the nearest town?
k Could you tell me / Do you know if they have booked a meeting room?

4 Students work with a partner to do the exercise. Make sure Student A first explains the problem with the server to Student B, so that it is clear why the information must be given over the phone. Student A repeats the polite questions in 3 to get the information. Student B will find all the information to answer Student A's questions on page 136.

ANSWERS

a It leaves at 19.55.
b It leaves from Terminal 2.
c It's about 40 miles.

d One hour
e Avis
f Either a Range Rover 3.6 or a Jeep Grand Cherokee
g Yes, you do.
h You are staying at The Lodge.
i Yes, it's a five-star hotel.
j It's 20 miles from the nearest town.
k Yes, all the rooms (including the meeting room) have been booked for the whole week.

> **Language links** ▶
>
> Direct students to the *Language links* section on page 25, which has more information on the differences between direct and polite questions, and practice exercises to help students form polite statements and questions.

Telephone frustrations

In this section, students look at the kinds of things which make callers frustrated when they telephone a company. Students complete items in a list, then decide which ones are the most frustrating.

Warm-up

Focus students' attention on the photos on this page. Ask them to describe the expression on the man's face in the second photo and to say how they think he feels. Ask students if they ever feel like this at work.

1 Before they do the exercise, elicit from students what kind of things make them feel frustrated at work or in their personal lives. You could compile a class list of the most frustrating things. Elicit or focus attention on frustrating things to do with the telephone. Then students do the completion exercise individually. Check answers with the class.

ANSWERS

a play   b get   c take   d put   e transfer; repeat   f listen
g get; call   h return   i get

2 Students work with a partner or as a class to decide which of the five problems in 1 are the most frustrating. Then students turn to page 136 to check what the survey says. Ask how many students agree with the survey. Ask students if they have any useful tactics either for dealing with their frustration or for dealing with the person or company that is causing it.

3 Students answer the questions with a partner. Encourage them to compare their answers with other pairs or in small groups.

4 Ask students to read the article and find out how the author answers the questions in 3. Ask them if they found any of the information in the article surprising, and whether they think their own company has a similar problem with bad call-handling. Encourage students who have had their calls badly handled to tell the class what happened and how they felt.

ANSWERS

a It is still very important.
b transferring a call, placing a call on hold, dealing with angry callers, responding to enquiries about correspondence, using a caller's name and taking messages correctly
c Yes, it does.

5 Ask students to discuss the statement with a partner and decide whether or not they agree. Have a class feedback session. If students have differing views, you might like to ask them to prepare arguments on one side or the other, to present to the class in a mini-debate in the next lesson. Encourage them to cite personal experience to back up their arguments.

> **1:1** Try to initiate a debate with your student by finding out his / her views on the question and putting forward arguments for the opposing point of view. Prepare arguments for both points of view in advance so that you are ready to respond, whatever line your student chooses to take.

6 **1.10–1.15** Tell students that they are going to hear extracts from six telephone calls. As parts of the listening script are given in 7, tell them to cover this part of the page before they listen. Remind them of the skills listed in paragraph 2 of the article on page 21, then ask them to listen and match the relevant skills with each extract.

ANSWERS

a Placing calls on hold.
b Taking messages correctly and using a caller's name.
c Dealing with angry callers and using a caller's name.
d Transferring a call.
e Responding to enquiries about correspondence.
f Using a caller's name and avoiding the use of informal expressions.

 1.10

A

A: Can I have extension 305, please?
B: I'm afraid the line is engaged. Will you hold?

 1.11

B

A: Could I just check that? You need 50 units by Friday, and Mr Johansson can contact you on 943 694 726?
B: Yes, that's correct.
A: Right, Mr Smith. I'll give him the message as soon as he's free.

1.12

C

A: ... and it really isn't good enough.
B: Yes, Mr Wright. I understand what you're saying and I apologize for the error. As soon as Mr Downs is back, I'll ask him to get in contact with you. I'm really sorry about this.
A: Right, thank you. I realize it's not your fault.

1.13

D

A: Could I have the sales department, please?

B: One moment, please. Just putting you through now.

 1.14

E

A: Shonagh Clark speaking.

B: Hello, I'm phoning about your letter of 12th June.

A: Have you got a reference number, please?

1.15

F

A: This is Jorgen Bode here. Could I speak to Jean Simmons, please?

B: Oh, I'm sorry, Mr Bode, but Ms Simmons isn't in the office right now. Can I ask her to call you back? Or I can contact her on her mobile if it's urgent?

7 1.10–1.15 Students read the gapped conversations, then listen to the extracts again to complete the missing phrases. Students could then practise the conversations with a partner.

ANSWERS

a extension; is engaged

b just check that; give him the message

c I apologize for; I'm really sorry

d putting you through

e phoning about

f isn't in the office; contact her on her mobile

8 Students match the words and phrases with a partner. Check answers with the class. To make the exercise more interactive, you could ask one student to say the correct question or statement, and another student to provide a suitable reply. This exercise contains language that students will find very useful when they make their own telephone calls in English. Draw their attention to the use of polite questions in the first two sections. You might like to point out that the addition of *please* at the end of all the questions would make them even more polite, and that *please* is used (and expected) in English a lot more than its equivalents in some other languages. Finally, encourage students to add three of their own expressions to the list. Go around monitoring and assisting while they do this.

ANSWERS

Could you put me through to (Accounts)?

Could you repeat that, please?

Could you read that back to me?

Could you give me your name?

Could you take a message?

Could I leave a message?

Could I speak to Mr Wilson?

Could I have extension 103, please?

Could I check that?

Could I go over that again?

I'm phoning to see if you could attend a meeting on the 20th.

I'm phoning about your advertisement.

I'm phoning to confirm our meeting.

I'm phoning for some information.

I'm phoning to make an appointment.

Direct students to the *Language links* section on page 24, where they will find more on telephone phrases. When they have completed exercise 2 on page 24, they could practise the conversations in pairs. It is a good idea to sit students back-to-back while practising telephone conversations, so they can't see each other's faces and have to listen carefully to what their partner says.

Sales contacts

In this section, students practise taking down information from phone calls.

1 1.16 Begin by focusing attention on the form and finding out if students' companies use similar forms. What kind of information do their own forms require? Make sure students read the form thoroughly, so that they know what kind of information they are listening for. Then play the recording for them to complete the form.

ANSWERS

a 54 Eisenhower Lane North, Lombard

b customer support department

c 630 953 3340

d manual

e just over 100

f 20,000

g 10,000

h 30,000

i A5

j samples

k Friday, 16th

 1.16

A: Hello, could I speak to Barry White, please?

B: Speaking. How can I help you?

A: Hello, Mr White. My name is Schmidt, from AMC Elevator.

B: Yes, I think I've heard of you.

A: I'm in charge of the customer support department. I'm phoning to ask for an estimate. It's for a service manual we're preparing.

B: Oh, yes. I don't think we've done anything for you before.

A: No, that's right. We're in the process of updating all our manuals. If the price is right, it will mean quite a lot of work.

B: I see. Well, could you give me the details, then?

A: Yes, it's for a manual of just over 100 pages.

B: 100 pages. Could you tell me what size?

A: It's in A5. We want to print 20,000. But I'd like estimates for 10,000 and 30,000 as well.

B: Okay. Is it in colour?

A: No, it's in black and white. Mainly text. The cover is in colour, though. I can put it all on a memory stick for you. Is that all right?

B: Yes, that would be perfect. Could I just read my notes back?

A: Yes, go ahead.

B: You want quotes for print runs of 10,000, 20,000 and 30,000 of an A5 100-page manual in black and white. The cover is in colour and you'll be supplying the material on a memory stick.

A: That's right.

B: Would you like me to visit you with some samples?

A: Yes, okay.

B: Would tomorrow morning suit you?

A: No, I'm out of the office tomorrow. How about Friday? About ten o'clock?

B: Friday … the 16th … at ten. That's fine. I'll bring the estimates with me and we can discuss the details then.

A: Fine.

B: Oh, could you give me the address?

A: 54 Eisenhower Lane North, Lombard.

B: And your telephone number?

A: 630 953 3340.

B: 630 953 3340. Right. Maybe you could give me your email?

A: Yes, it's schmidt@amcelevator.com.

B: Can I just check that? schmidt, at amcelevator, dot, com.

A: Yes, that's right.

B: Okay, then, Mr Schmidt. See you on Friday.

A: Great. Goodbye for now.

B: Bye.

2 Give students plenty of time to read the situations and decide what they are going to say. Remind them of all the useful telephone language they have studied in this unit and encourage them to put it into practice. Discourage them from writing out a script, but allow them to jot down prompts if they find this helpful. This is another situation where it is a good idea to have students sitting back to back. They will then have to concentrate on their own form and what is being said to them, and will be unable to glance at their partner's information for help.

 1:1 Take one of the roles yourself so that your student can practise telephoning for information and taking notes.

In company interviews Units 1–3
Encourage students to watch the interview and complete the worksheet.

Language links

ANSWERS

Vocabulary

Numbers

1 a three hundred and twenty-one
 b sixty-nine per cent
 c three thousand, four hundred and twenty-eight
 d three million pounds
 e nine dollars, thirty-nine cents
 f twenty-four million, six hundred and seventy-eight thousand, nine hundred and two

Telephone phrases

2 1 Hello, BDC Electronics.
 2 Oh, good morning. Could I speak to Peter White, please?
 3 Just one moment … I'm sorry, there's no answer.
 4 Oh, dear. I'm phoning for some information. It's quite urgent. Do you know where I can contact him?
 5 No, sorry. I'm afraid I don't. Can I take a message?
 6 Yes, please. Could you ask him to phone John Clarkson from Duraplex? He has the phone number.
 7 Yes, of course. Could I just check your name? John Clark from Duraplex.
 8 No, it's Clarkson. He knows what it's about.
 9 Oh, sorry, Mr Clarkson. I'll tell him as soon as he's available.
 10 Thank you. Goodbye.

3 a dialled the wrong number
 b put me through
 c bad line
 d engaged
 e hold
 f You're through
 g Could I speak to
 h Can I take a message
 i This is
 j call me

4 a 4 b 6 c 1 d 3 e 5 f 2

5 a 8 b 4 c 1 d 6 e 10 f 12 g 3 h 2 i 5 j 7 k 9 l 11

Grammar

Practice 1

a Could you tell me if she got my message?
b Do you know when he will be back?
c Do you know how long it takes?
d Can you remember what time the bus leaves?
e Do you know what this word means?
f What do you think he wants to know?
g I've no idea what the time is.

Practice 2

a Do you know what time the meeting begins?
b Could you tell me how much the hotel is?
c Do you know why he is angry?
d Can you tell me if there is a restaurant car on the train?
e Can you tell me where I can park the car?
f Can you remember if/whether the office is near the town centre?

04 Networking

Learning objectives

This unit is about networking – the skill of making useful business contacts by socializing at conferences, meetings, parties and so on. Students practise the kinds of questions that people ask when they are making small talk. Furthermore they learn how to describe other people.

In this first section, students listen to two people making small talk in a hotel bar. They answer questions about what is said and complete the questions that are asked in the conversation. They then practise forming their own questions to find out information about the person sitting next to them.

Digital resources: Unit 4

Online Workbook; Extension worksheets; Glossary; Student's Book answer key; Student's Book listening script; Fast-track map

Warm-up

Elicit or explain the meaning of *gossip*. Then ask students to stand in a line. Whisper a piece of gossip to the first person in the line. That person whispers it to the next person, and so on, until it has reached the end of the line.

No one is allowed to ask for a repetition of what has been said. The final person tells the others what he / she has heard. Usually the facts will have changed substantially, and students can have fun seeing how gossip and rumours can move further and further away from the truth, the more people are involved in the telling of them.

Focus attention on the quotation and ask students if they agree with it.

Then move the discussion on to networking. Point out that a lot of the conversations students will study in this unit are examples of *networking*. Write this word on the board and elicit that it refers to making useful business contacts by talking to people at meetings, conferences, on planes, etc. A *network* is a collection of things that are connected, and *networking* often involves introducing people to each other or getting introductions to people through contacts you have already made. Find out how often the students have to do it in their work, and whether or not they enjoy it.

 1:1 Ask your student if he / she agrees with the quotation. Discuss what qualities a good conversationalist has.

1 Students discuss the questions with a partner. Have a class feedback session to compare answers.

2 **1.17** Explain that students are about to listen to a conversation in a bar between two businessmen. Elicit ideas about the kinds of things the two men might talk about.

Ask students to read the questions in 2 before you play the recording, so that they know exactly what information they are listening for. Check answers with the class.

ANSWERS

a He works in the marketing department of a retail company that sells leisure goods.
b He is a sales manager for a large Dutch clothing firm called Verweij Fashion.
c No, they don't.

🔘 **1.17**

Conversation 1

A: Hello, do you mind if I join you?

B: Er, no, not at all.

A: How do you do? My name's Rick Van Looy.

B: Hi. Pleased to meet you. I'm Florent Rondele.

A: Are you from around here, then?

B: No, but my company has a store in town. Actually, I live in France.

A: So, what do you do, Florent?

B: I'm in marketing. I work for a retail company. We deal mainly in leisure goods.

A: Do you mean sports equipment?

B: Well, both sports and casual wear. Clothes, shoes, accessories, stuff like that. We have stores in several countries.

A: Sounds like a big operation. How many stores have you got?

B: Nearly 50 in total. And what line of business are you in, Rick?

A: Well, quite similar really. I'm a sales manager for a large Dutch clothing firm, Verweij Fashion – do you know it?

B: Yes, of course. Are you opening a store here, then?

A: Yes, we're looking at possible sites at the moment.

B: Hmm. That can be a slow process. Rick, do you fancy something to drink?

A: Erm, yeah, thanks.

B: Come on, then. There's a table free over there.

---

3 🔘 **1.18** Explain that students are going to listen to a second conversation, with different speakers and a different setting. Again, make sure students read the questions before you play the recording. Check answers with the class.

ANSWERS

a They are on a plane. (clues: *it's a long flight*; *do we land soon?*)
b Probably a pen (clues: *it was on the floor*; *she was looking for it* in order to finish a crossword)
c Bangkok
d One of them lives there. The other is going there on business to visit a supplier.

1.18

Conversation 2

A: Excuse me, does this belong to you?

B: Oh, thank you very much.

A: It was on the floor.

B: Yes, I was looking for it just now. I wanted to finish this crossword. I'm feeling a bit groggy, actually.

A: Yes, it's a long flight.

B: Isn't it? Have you got the time?

A: Yes, it's ... erm ... just after midnight.

B: So, do we land soon?

A: Yes, in about half an hour.

B: Oh, good. Do you know Bangkok?

A: Yes, I live there. Is this your first trip there?

B: Yes, it is actually.

A: On business, I suppose?

B: Yes, I'm visiting a supplier.

A: Oh, really? I wonder if I ...

4 **1.17–1.18** Before listening again, ask students to look through the table of questions and try to complete the gaps. Then play the recordings again. You may need to play them several times and pause between the two conversations to give students time to complete the gaps. After checking answers with the class, ask students to suggest a suitable response to each question.

ANSWERS

c What **do you** do?

d **Do** you **mean** sports equipment?

e How many stores **have you** got?

f What line of business **are you** in?

g Do **you** know it?

h Are you **opening** a store here, then?

i **Do** you **fancy** something to drink?

j Does **this** belong **to you**?

k **Have** you **got** the time?

l Do **we land** soon?

m Do **you know** Bangkok?

n **Is** this your first trip there?

5 Students write the questions with a partner. After checking their answers on page 130, ask one student to read out a question and another to provide the answer. In this way, students will hear the questions and answers in the context of a conversation, and it should make the structures easier to remember. You could ask students to follow this up by taking turns to ask each other the questions and giving answers which are true for them.

ANSWERS

a Who do you work for?

b Where is your company based?

c Where are you staying?

d Do you speak (German)?

e Who is (Alex) talking to?

f What do you do? / What's your job?

g Have you got any children? / Do you have any children?

h Where are you from? / Where do you come from?

i Are you married?

j Do you play golf?

k Do you know (Adriana Bellini)?

6 In this exercise, students get the chance to put into practice what they have learned. See who can find out the most information about their partner in the time allowed, but emphasize to students that the art of small talk does not lie in grilling people about their backgrounds. Questions need to be put gently and answers responded to with polite interest and reciprocal information about oneself.

 Ask your student the questions and encourage him / her to ask you similar questions. Try to structure this as a proper conversation, not an inquisition or a conversational ping-pong match. Demonstrate how questions can be put gently and how answers can be responded to and can be supplemented by information about oneself or a reciprocal question.

Talking about other people

Conversations which focus solely on the exchange of personal information between two people are unlikely to be sustained for long. This section introduces students to talking about other people. They first put a conversation in order, then they examine some of the language used in it and some alternative expressions which could have been used. Finally, they practise talking about other people, using a chart to provide the core information.

Warm-up

Find out from students if they have ever been introduced by someone else to someone they wanted to meet. Was the introduction successful?

1 **1.19** Students work with a partner to order the conversation. When they have listened and checked their answers, ask one pair to perform the conversation for the class.

ANSWERS

See listening script below.

 1.19

Conversation 3

A: Do you know Jan Nowacki?

B: Yes, isn't he Director of Business Development at Pepsico in Europe?

A: Not any longer. Now he's the Public Relations Manager at the National Bank of Poland.

B: The National Bank of Poland, that's interesting. Do you have any contact with him in your work?

A: Not really, but I occasionally play golf with him.

B: What's he like?

A: He's a nice guy. You'd like him.

 Take one of the roles yourself and read the conversation with your student. Remember to work on intonation and sentence and word stress, so that the conversation sounds natural.

2 Students identify the parts of the conversation in 1 that could be replaced with the given expressions. If you have time, ask them to roleplay the conversation with a partner, using the new expressions where appropriate.

ANSWERS

a Do you know
b Isn't he …
c Not any longer
d What's he like?
e You'd like him.

3 Go through the instructions with the class. Make sure everyone understands that the jobs the people used to do are shown in the two columns on the left of the table, and their present positions by the two columns on the right. Establish that one person has retired, and elicit who it is (Dennis Sexton). Check also that students understand the phrases in the *Useful language* box. As students practise their conversations in pairs, go around offering help and encouragement. Make a note of any particularly good conversations which can be performed for the class.

4 With a different partner, students have the same type of conversation that they had in 3, but using people that they really know. Again, make a note of any interesting conversations which can be performed for the class.

WORKPLACE SCENARIO

A Passing the buck

Learning objectives

This scenario is based on the issue of communication breakdowns in the workplace. Students begin by reading an article on the causes of communication problems at work, and discussing the causes of these problems and their own experience of them. They then watch a video in which an HR director talks about a communication breakdown that is affecting her work. Discussion of this problem and what can be done about it leads up to a simulated meeting in which students assume the roles of the two people involved and try to resolve the problem. They then watch another video and compare their solutions to those shown.

Digital resources: Workplace Scenario A

In company in action A1–A2 and worksheet; Extension worksheets; Glossary; Student's Book answer key; Student's Book listening script; Fast-track map

Warm-up

Focus attention on the definition of *pass the buck* and brainstorm situations in which people try to pass the buck. You might also like to introduce the phrase *The buck stops here,* made famous by US President Harry S Truman, who had it as a sign on his desk – indicating his willingness to take responsibility for what happened under his leadership and his refusal to try to shift the blame onto other people.

1 Focus attention on the article and explain that it is about communication breakdowns in the workplace – times when misunderstandings between colleagues occur, causing resentment and frustration. Give students time to read the article. Answer any questions about difficult vocabulary. Then go through the questions with the class before asking students to discuss them with a partner. Have a class feedback session in which students can share their opinions and experiences.

2 📹 **A1** Go through the instructions, the questions and the various options with the class, then play the video and ask students to choose the correct options.

ANSWERS

a iii b i

📹 **A1**
Part one
Serena: Hi, Vanessa.
Vanessa: Hello.
S: Have you got a minute?
V: Sure. Do you want a grape?

S: No, thanks. It's about the new website. Are you the best person to speak to?
V: If it's about marketing or design, then yes.
S: Well, I'm not sure exactly. I think the website looks great, you and Eric have done a really good job, but ... what's happened to the recruitment section?
V: Nothing. It's still there.
S: I know, but I thought we planned an online application form and CV upload facility.
V: Ah. Yes. You'll need to talk to Eric about that. He's responsible for anything technical.
S: Oh, I see. Well, I don't mind who does it, but I really think it needs to be added soon.
V: Absolutely. Eric will be able to sort it out for you.
S: Okay, I'll talk to him now. Thanks Vanessa.
V: No problem.

Part two
Serena: Hi, Eric, sorry to bother you at lunchtime. How are things?
Eric: Really busy. I haven't even had time to eat yet.
S: Just a quick question then. I noticed that the online application form and CV upload facility aren't on the new website. Can you add them for me when you get time?
E: Marketing.
S: Sorry, marketing?
E: Marketing. That's content, and anything like that is a marketing issue. You need to talk to Vanessa.
S: But I just spoke to her, and she told me to ask you.
E: Nope, sorry. The IT department doesn't do content. We're more backend.
S: Okay, if you're sure.
E: Very sure.
S: Right. Bye then.

Part three
Serena: Vanessa, hi! I'm glad I caught you. Can I have a word?
Vanessa: Okay, as long as it's quick.
S: Well, I spoke to Eric and he told me my problem with the recruitment section of the website is a marketing issue.
V: Did he? That doesn't sound right.
S: He told me to ask you.
V: Sorry Serena, but I think he might be trying to pass the buck.
S: Well, I really don't mind who does it, but it is very important ...
V: You know what these techie types are like. It's definitely his area. Sorry, got to rush.
S: But ...

3 Students discuss the questions with a partner. Have a class feedback session to check answers and compare opinions and experiences.

ANSWERS

a Neither Vanessa nor Eric is willing to take responsibility for the problem that has been identified with the website. Neither Vanessa nor Eric treats Serena with respect.

b Students' own answers

 1:1 Ask your student to talk about his / her experience of passing the buck – either when they have experienced this in other people or when they have avoided taking responsibility themselves. Be prepared to describe experiences of your own to help the conversation along.

4 Go through the instructions with students. Allow them time to read the email and decide individually what they think about Joe's advice, and whether there is any different advice they would give to Serena. Have a class feedback session to compare opinions.

5 Tell students they are going to roleplay the meeting between Serena and Vanessa with their partners from 3. Once they have turned their respective pages, make sure students have understood the information and instructions. Encourage them to use as many of the useful phrases as they can during their roleplays.

6 Ask students to individually complete the FEEDBACK: Self-assessment section on page 132, then discuss their answers with their partner from 5. Ask students if they found anything surprising in exercises 5 and 6.

7 📹 **A2** Play the video so that students can see what actually happened in Serena and Vanessa's meeting. Then ask them to swap roles and repeat their roleplay, again incorporating as many of the useful phrases as they can.

📹 **A2**

Serena: Thanks for meeting with me, Vanessa.

Vanessa: No problem. Would you like a cookie?

S: No thanks.

V: Are you sure? They're delicious.

S: Thank you, I'm fine.

V: So, what did you want to talk about?

S: It's about the recruitment section of the website. Now, there was supposed to be an online application form and a facility for people to upload their CVs. When I asked you to do it, you told me it was Eric's job, but Eric told me to ask you. He said it was a marketing issue.

V: Yes, there's been a mix-up.

S: That's right, and now I'm stuck in the middle. We really need to get this sorted out; the website is a very important tool for the HR department. Now,

am I right in thinking that you are the person with overall responsibility for the website?

V: Yes, that's right. There's been a misunderstanding. I thought Eric was doing it because of the CV upload facility, which needs some backend programming. But he thought I was doing it because the application form is part of the website's content.

S: Okay, but when can we get this fixed?

V: I'm going to have a meeting with Eric this afternoon so we can schedule getting both parts of the section completed. I think we can agree on what to do next, and have the CV upload facility available by the end of the week.

S: That would be great. I also think you should both clarify your roles, we don't want this to happen again.

V: I agree; resolving this problem is in everyone's interest.

S: It sounds like we've found a solution. I'll send you and Eric an email later to confirm what we've discussed.

V: Okay, that's fine. Are you sure you don't want a cookie?

S: Oh, go on then.

8 Focus attention on the beginning of Serena's email. Ask students to complete it. With weaker classes, you could offer more support by first brainstorming the points that Serena needs to include in her email, and writing them on the board. When students have finished, ask them to compare their emails with the one on page 136.

05 Internet histories

Learning objectives

This unit is about the past and future direction of the Internet. It starts by looking at the history of Angry Birds™, the successful app game which can be played on computers, mobile devices and games consoles. Students then answer a quiz on the history of the Internet and listen to a radio documentary before completing an article. They do more work on the structure of questions and finally write a short presentation on the history of their company, or one that they know.

The grammatical focus is on the Past Simple and time expressions, and the lexical focus is on business and the Internet verbs.

Digital resources: Unit 5

Online Workbook; Extension worksheets; Glossary; Phrase bank; Student's Book answer key; Student's Book listening script; Fast-track map; Quick progress test 1

In this first section, students complete a text on the popular game Angry Birds™, which uses the Present Simple to list the dates and events in the company's history. They then practise writing questions using the Past Simple.

Warm-up

Focus attention on the quotation and find out if any of the students understand it. Ask them to explain what an **app** is and what **the cloud** is (**app** = a piece of software that can be run on the Internet, a computer, a phone or other electronic device; **the cloud** = a way of delivering IT services in which resources are accessed from the internet rather than downloaded via a server).

1 Elicit the names of some apps that students have on their computers and phones. Have a class discussion about which apps are the most popular, and whether students think they are important in business.

2 **1.20** Find out how much students know about Angry Birds. Ask whether anyone has the app and, if so, how often they play it. If some students are unfamiliar with the game, ask a student who plays it to explain. (The game consists of birds attacking pigs who have stolen their eggs, by catapulting themselves towards various structures the pigs have built for protection.) Go through the questions before you play the recording, so that students know what information to listen out for. While you play the recording, tell students to cover the timeline history of Angry Birds in 3 so they are genuinely listening for information, not reading the text at the same time. Tell students to compare answers with a partner, then check answers with the class.

1.20

With over one billion downloads, Angry Birds™ is perhaps the largest mobile app success so far. It has been praised for its successful combination of addictive games, humorous style and low price. There are versions of Angry Birds for personal computers and games consoles, a market for merchandise featuring its characters, and even long-term plans for a feature film or television series. Here is its history.

In early 2009, a designer, Jaakko Iisalo, presented the idea for a new game to his colleagues at Finnish computer game developer, Rovio Entertainment. The game featured some angry-looking birds. They liked the basic idea, but decided to give the birds some pigs as an enemy because of an outbreak of swine flu at the time. They estimated the initial costs of developing the game were €100,000. After a long period of development, in December 2009, in partnership with Chillingo, Rovio published Angry Birds on Apple® App Store. In March 2010, Angry Birds achieved top-selling app status on the USA's App Store, where it stayed until October that year. Also in March, they launched a version of the game for Facebook. In October 2010, Rovio released the first version of the game for Android and experienced more than one million downloads in the first 24 hours and two million in its first weekend. Throughout 2010, versions for other platforms appeared. The company claimed revenues of over $100,000 a month just for the advertising on the free version of the game.

In December 2010, on the anniversary of its first release, Rovio announced over 50 million downloads, including 12 million on Apple's iOS devices and 10 million on Android.

In April 2011, the UK Appy Awards named Angry Birds as both the 'Best Game App' and 'App of the Year'. In May 2012, the different versions of the game reached the one billion-downloads mark. At the Electronic Entertainment Expo in Los Angeles in June 2012, Rovio and distribution partner Activision revealed plans to bring Angry Birds and two of its spin-off games (the Angry Birds Trilogy) to the PlayStation 3, Xbox® 360 and Nintendo 3DS systems, taking advantage of their unique features, such as glasses-free 3D visuals. It's been quite a success story!

3 **1.20** Ask students to complete as much of the timeline history as they can before you play the recording. Then play the recording to allow them to check their answers.

ANSWERS

a downloads   b merchandise   c colleagues
d costs   e partnership   f platforms   g revenues
h anniversary   i distribution   j spin-off

4 Focus attention on the pronunciation of the Past Simple verbs in the table. Make sure students understand that the *-ed* endings of regular Past Simple verbs are pronounced in three different ways, and model these sounds for the students. As a class or in pairs, ask students to write the Past Simple forms of the bold verbs in 3 under the correct headings in the table. While they are doing this, encourage them to say the Past Simple forms aloud so that they get a feel for what sounds right.

ANSWERS

Group 1: achieved, appeared, claimed, named, revealed
Group 2: liked, published, launched, released, announced, reached
Group 3: presented, estimated

Language links ▶

Direct students to the Grammar part of the *Language links* section on pages 35–36, for more information and practice on the Past Simple.

5 **1.20** Tell students to check their answers to 4 by listening to the recording again. (Explain that in the recording, the verbs in 4 are all in the Past Simple.) Then check answers with the class to make sure that the students put the verbs in the correct columns.

6 Focus attention on the example question. Elicit several other questions in the Past Simple to check that students can form it correctly. Tell students to write five of their own questions about the history of Angry Birds, working individually and using the text in 3 for ideas.

7 Tell students to work with a partner, taking turns to ask and answer their questions from 6. Make sure they are using the Past Simple in their answers.

 Prepare five questions about Angry Birds that you can ask your student. Be prepared to answer his / her questions using information from the text.

Who really invented the Internet?

In this section, students do a quiz on the early years of the Internet and then listen to a radio documentary about it and number events in the correct order. They continue their work on the Past Simple by completing an article on the birth of the Internet and by asking and answering questions on it. This develops into more work on the formation of questions, particularly those which have no subject.

Warm-up

Find out how important the Internet is in students' lives and whether they mainly use it for business or for pleasure. Ask them if they can remember sending their first email. When was it, and who did they send it to?

1 Put students in groups and ask them to discuss the questions, then report back to the class on what they found out.

 Be prepared to talk about your own use of the Internet with your student. If you have something to contribute to the conversation, your student will be more likely to be inspired to talk about his / her own experiences.

2 Students work with a partner to do the quiz before comparing their answers in small groups. Have a class feedback session to see how much consensus there is.

3 **1.21** Play the recording for students to check their answers in 2. Ask students if they found anything surprising.

ANSWERS

1 a   2 c   3 b   4 c   5 b

1.21

How old is the Internet? Different experts suggest different dates. It depends on what they understand the Internet to be.

We know that in 1965, the Advanced Research Projects Agency (ARPA), under the US Department of Defence, began work on a system to connect computers. They called the project ARPANET.

On September 2nd, 1969, in a laboratory at the University of California, Professor Leonard Kleinrock connected the first two machines. For many people, that day the Internet was born. The next month they sent the first message to a computer at Stanford University.

By January 1970, ARPANET connected computers in four American universities, and by the following year there were 23 in the system, connecting different universities and research institutes. In 1973, Ray Tomlinson sent the first email via ARPANET. In the same year the Net went international, connecting computers in England and Norway.

The next step was to connect different networks and to create an 'Internetwork'. In 1974, Bob Kahn and Vincent Cerf invented a software called TCP/IP that connected networks using different operating systems. On January 1st, 1983, this software became the universal language of the Internet – many experts think that this event was the real birth of the Internet because it made it possible to link different networks in one web.

More and more networks joined the system and the number of connected computers increased dramatically, from 10,000 in 1984 to 100,000 in 1987. By the early 1990s, the network was accessible to anyone in the world with a computer. In 1992, the number of hosts reached one million.

In 1993, two programmers, Marc Andreessen and Eric Bina, launched the first version of Mosaic – the first graphics-based browser of the type we all use today – which made the Internet an easy means to browse websites, get information and spread news.

4 🔘 **1.21** Go through the events with the class. Ask students to try to order the events from memory before they listen again. Then play the recording for students to check their answers.

ANSWERS

1 The Advanced Research Projects Agency starts work on ARPANET.
2 Professor Kleinrock connects two computers.
3 ARPANET links four American universities.
4 Ray Tomlinson sends the first email.
5 Bob Kahn and Vincent Cerf invent software for connecting computers on the Internet.
6 A 'universal language' of the Internet is established.
7 The first Internet browser becomes available.

5 If students are not confident with Past Simple verb forms, go through the verbs in the box first and elicit the Past Simple form of each verb. Then tell students to complete the article.

ANSWERS

a began b called c connected d connected e sent
f invented g became h made i increased j reached
k launched

Language links

Direct students to Practice 6 in the *Language links* section on page 36 for more practice of Past Simple verb forms.

6 🔘 **1.21** Play the recording again for students to check their answers in 5, then answer any questions about difficult vocabulary in the article. Ask them how much of the information in the article they already knew.

7 Students work with a partner to form Past Simple questions from the prompts, then ask and answer the questions. You could then ask them to add two extra questions of their own.

ANSWERS

a When did Professor Kleinrock connect the first two computers? (On September 2nd, 1969.)
b Where did they send the first message? (To a computer at Stanford University.)
c What did Ray Tomlinson send in 1973? (The first email.)
d What did Bob Kahn and Vincent Cerf invent? (Software that allowed networks using different operating systems to connect to each other.)
e When did TCP/IP become the universal language? (On January 1st, 1983.)
f How much did the Internet grow between 1984 and 1987? (It grew tenfold.)

 Tell your student to form the questions and then ask you them.

8 Focus attention on the two structure boxes. Elicit two more examples of questions using these two structures. Encourage students to use these questions to quiz each other.

9 Students work with a partner, taking turns to ask and answer questions based on the chart. As an extra activity, you could ask them to write five questions using the two structures in 7, about either the history of the Internet or the history of their own company.

Language links

The *Language links* section on page 35 has more information about Past Simple questions, and Practice 3 on page 36 provides more practice of Past Simple questions.

10 Go through the example with the class, perhaps asking a pair of students to read it aloud. Emphasize the importance of follow-up questions, which are used to keep a conversation going, but remind them that one shouldn't barrage people with questions either. (And that it is important to listen and respond to what is said in answer to a question.) With weaker students, check that pairs have matched up the verbs and phrases correctly, and can put all the verbs into the Past Simple, before they ask each other the questions.

 Take the role of either Speaker A or Speaker B. When it is your turn to ask a question, remember to use a follow-up question to find out more details. Be sure to respond to your student's answers.

Company history

In this section, students get the opportunity to put into practice everything they have learned in this unit by producing a short presentation about their own company's history. Reassure them that they can use a different company if they prefer or make up the details if they are unfamiliar with the history of a real company.

Warm-up

Find out from students how much they know about their own company's history. Do they know when the company was founded and by whom? Has it always been involved in the same kind of business? What major events have taken place over the years?

Check that students understand the meaning of the verbs in the box. Go through the items in the list and then give students time to prepare their presentations. If your students work for the same company, you could brainstorm some facts about the company with the whole class, before asking students to work individually on their presentations.

Allow time for all students to make their presentations to the rest of the class, and encourage the listening students to think of questions that they can ask each presenter at the end. This will ensure that they pay attention to all the presentations and will make the presenters feel that their work has been appreciated.

Language links

ANSWERS

Vocabulary

Business verbs and the Internet

Suggested answers

a became b release c develop d claim e estimated
f reach g announced h downloaded i presented j achieve

Grammar
Practice 1

a worked b stopped c lived d started e used
f travelled g dropped h carried i tipped j married
k planned l reached m arrived n fitted o visited
p called q increased r liked

Practice 2

a told b said c got d gave e took f put g made
h did i went j came k wrote l had

Practice 3

a Where did you go on your last business trip?
b When did he set up the company?
c What did they start selling last year?
d Why did the product sell well at first?
e How did they make a profit?
f How long did he work for ICI?
g Who did you speak to at the conference?
h Who invented the mobile phone?
i How many people work in the Lille factory?
j How did you travel from Munich to Berlin?

Practice 4

a at; ago b X c On d X e When; for / at f at
g for h in i at; in; at; in j X k when

Practice 5

Suggested answers

a Steve Jobs didn't co-found Google, he co-founded Apple®.
b The Wall Street Crash didn't start a worldwide economic boom, it started an economic depression.
c The six European states didn't sign the Treaty of Madrid, they signed the Treaty of Rome.
d The 11 member states of the European Union didn't adopt the pound as a common currency, they adopted the euro.
e Engineers at Apple didn't produce the Android smartphone, they produced the iPhone.
f Mark Zuckerberg didn't invent Twitter, he invented Facebook.

06 Orders

Learning objectives

This unit is about dealing with orders and includes work on different types of correspondence, particularly emails. It begins with a common use of email: to confirm an order received over the telephone. With the growth of email and the decline in letter writing, many native speakers of English have relaxed their writing style, and with increased informality has come an increased tendency towards inaccuracy and an apparent tolerance of grammatical errors. However, this unit contains a warning about the financial consequences of bad writing skills in the workplace, which may not be tolerated as much as people may think.

The grammatical focus is on *will* for unplanned decisions, and the lexical focus is on business communication.

Digital resources: Unit 6

Online Workbook; Extension worksheets; Glossary; Phrase bank; Student's Book answer key; Student's Book listening script; Fast-track map

Warm-up

Focus attention on the quotation from Confucius and ask students to answer the question that follows it. Have a class discussion on the degree of importance attached to errors in their industry and whether they think there is greater tolerance of error now than there used to be.

In this first section, students listen to a telephone conversation about an order. They answer questions and practise the conversation using prompts. They then complete an email confirming the order. Further exercises explore what happens when something goes wrong with this order and how the people involved deal with the problem.

Warm-up

Ask students if they have any experience of taking orders by telephone and if anything has ever gone wrong with the order. Encourage them to tell the class what happened and how they dealt with it. Find out what the procedure is in their company for accepting orders by phone. Is a confirmation letter needed? Do they have to fill out a particular form?

1 1.22 Go through the questions with students before you play the recording, so that they know what information to listen out for.

ANSWERS

a John Bird
c SG 94321
e 22nd June
b Hydraulic pumps
d Five
f It's for a new customer.

 1.22

A: SAG, can I help you?

B: Yes, could I speak to John Bird?

A: I'm afraid he's not in the office right now. Can I take a message?

B: Oh dear! It's an urgent order – we need five hydraulic pumps by 22nd June.

A: Just a minute. Could you tell me your name, please?

B: Yes, I'm sorry. It's Elena Moretti, from Stern Hydraulics in Switzerland.

A: Right, I'll take down the details and get John to contact you. Did you say five units?

B: Yes, the reference is SG 94321.

A: SG 94321 – five units.

B: Yes, that's right. But the important thing is the delivery date – 22nd June.

A: I don't think that will be a problem.

B: Good, it's for a new customer.

A: I see. Right, when John comes in, I'll tell him immediately. Could you confirm the order by email?

B: Yes, of course. Thanks very much.

A: You're welcome. Goodbye.

B: Goodbye.

2 The use of prompts here is designed to help students to construct the same conversation that they heard in 1, but without reading it straight off the page. The more you can get students' eyes off the page and looking at each other when they practise conversations, the better they will sound and the more fluent they will become. Encourage them to look at each other as much as possible when they speak and to listen carefully to what their partner says. Check the answers by having one confident pair perform their conversation for the class. Ask the others to put their hands up if they disagree with a particular sentence.

ANSWERS

See listening script 1.22 above.

---

3 Ask students to work individually to complete the email, then compare answers with a partner before you check answers with the class. Accept any grammatically correct answers that fit the information on the recording.

ANSWERS

a my conversation   b to confirm   c five
d 22 June   e new

---

4 Students work with a partner to complete the conversation. Encourage them to read it aloud when they have finished to check whether it sounds correct and makes sense.

5 1.23 Play the recording for students to check their answers in 4.

ANSWERS

Could I speak to
Is that
phoning
it's quite
worry; all the details
good; worried
help you
more business
in touch

 1.23

A: Could I speak to Elena Moretti, please?

B: Speaking. Is that John?

A: Yes. Hello, Elena. I'm just phoning back about your order.

B: Yes, it's quite urgent; I hope you can help.

A: Don't worry. I've got all the details in your email. No problem – we're happy to help.

B: That's good. I was quite worried about it.

A: It should be fine. Can I help you with anything else?

B: No, thank you. I hope we get more business from this customer.

A: Yes, of course. Okay, I'll be in touch. Bye for now.

B: Goodbye.

6 When students have identified the error in the order confirmation, ask them to speculate on how Elena felt when she received this document and why. What do they think she will do next? For homework, you could ask them to write a short telephone conversation or email from Elena to John Bird telling him about the mistake.

ANSWER

The delivery date is wrong – it should be 22 June.

7 **1.24** Students work with a partner to put the conversation in order. Then play the recording for them to check their answers. Students can also look at page 131 to check, and they can use the script there to practise the conversation with their partner. If students did the homework suggested in 6, ask them to compare their work with what Elena actually said in her telephone conversation with John Bird's colleague.

ANSWER

See Listening script below.

 1.24

A: SAG, can I help you?

B: Yes, this is Elena Moretti from Stern Hydraulics. Could I speak to John Bird, please?

A: Oh, hello, Elena. I'm afraid John isn't here at the moment. Can I take a message?

B: Yes, he sent me an order confirmation – the reference is DH010601 – but the delivery date is wrong.

A: Oh, dear. Can you give me the details?

B: Yes, it says 7th July, but the agreed delivery date was 22nd June. It's really important.

A: I see. Well, I'll tell him as soon as he comes in.

B: Thank you. I'm not at all happy about this. A lot depends on this order.

A: Right, Elena, leave it with me. I'm terribly sorry about this.

B: No, it's not your fault. Just ask John to phone me.

A: All right, then. Bye for now.

B: Goodbye.

8 When students have written their emails, ask them to compare them with a partner or in small groups.

SUGGESTED ANSWER

Dear Elena

I'm sorry I missed your call. I have checked our correspondence and I agree that you are absolutely right about the delivery date. I apologize for the mistake.

I have spoken to our production department, and they are giving your order top priority. As a result, I can confirm that the delivery date will be June 22nd.

Once again, please accept my apologies for the mistake.
Best wishes
John

Language links

Direct students to the *Language links* section on page 42, where they will find a practice activity with more useful words connected to the vocabulary of business communication, and a crossword using vocabulary from this unit.

9 Before putting students in pairs to do the roleplay, go through the situation with the class. Ask them for some words to describe how they think Elena feels, and how they think John feels. Elicit if this kind of thing has ever happened to them. Students then begin the roleplay. Go around offering help and encouragement where necessary. Note down any particularly successful exchanges and ask those students to perform their conversation to the class.

 Ask your student to choose one of the roles and be prepared to take the other one yourself.

Correspondence

In this second section, students discuss the importance of accuracy in writing, then read an article on the implications to a company of its employees not being able to write well. They then read a series of emails and correct the mistakes in punctuation, grammar and style.

Warm-up

Ask students if grammatical mistakes matter in their own language. Are standards of writing in their own language declining and, if so, do they think the development of email has contributed to this decline? Find out if formal grammar is still taught in schools in their country, and what people's attitudes are to correct spelling and punctuation.

1 Ask students to discuss the questions with a partner. Have a class feedback session to compare opinions.

2 Allow students plenty of time to read the article. Highlight the part at the end and ask them to say whether or not they agree with the bosses in the survey. When they have finished, you could ask them to try to summarize the main point of the article in one sentence. Alternatively, write a gapped version of this summary on the board and ask students to complete it: *While people, particularly the younger generation, are not too [concerned] about mistakes in the emails they [send], they are intolerant of [mistakes / errors] in the emails they [receive], and this could be costing companies a lot of [business / money].*

3 Students work with a partner to find and correct the mistakes. Discourage them from looking at the corrected emails on page 144 before they have finished. Remind them to underline any phrases that they think are useful and which they might like to use in their own emails.

ANSWERS

See Student's Book page 144

On-the-spot decisions

In this section, students listen to a telephone conversation in which an on-the-spot decision is made. They look at the use of *will* + infinitive for decisions made at the time of speaking. They then practise dialogues in which one person offers a problem and the other an on-the-spot solution.

Warm-up

In the dialogue in 1, students will hear someone dictating his email address over the phone. It might be a good idea to make sure at this point that students can give their own email addresses correctly, spelling out any difficult words and pointing out anything that is spelled as one word. You could write your own email address on the board first and read it out to the class to demonstrate how it is done.

1 **1.25** Make sure students have read the questions before you play the recording so that they know what information to listen out for. You may need to play the recording a second time so that they can note down any answers they missed the first time.

ANSWERS

a He wants to speak to Diego Martin.
b Because he hasn't replied to his text message.
c Because he needs a copy of a certificate for customs.
d He will email him a copy of the certificate as a pdf.
e jim.jfa@ciclosciclone.net

1.25

A: CiclosCiclone, can I help you?
B: Yes, I'm phoning from Ballyclare, in Northern Ireland. Could I speak to Diego Martin, please?
A: I'm afraid he's out of the office right now. Can I help you?

B: Well, I sent him a text message and he hasn't replied. It's really quite urgent.
A: Can you tell me what it's about?
B: It's a bit complicated to explain. I need a copy of a certificate for customs. Maybe he didn't get my message. Can I just check his mobile – 07636 746384?
A: Let me check. Yes, that's the right number. Listen, why don't you send the details to me by email and I'll send you a copy of the certificate as an attached pdf?
B: Yes, that's a good idea. What's your email address?
A: Jim, that's J-I-M, dot, J-F-A, at CiclosCiclone, dot, net. CiclosCiclone is all one word.
B: Can I just check that? Jim, dot, JFA, at CiclosCiclone, dot, net.
A: Yes, that's right.
B: Great. I'll deal with the email straight away. By the way, my name's David, David Holmbrook. And you are, Jim ...?
A: Kutz, Jim Kutz. Don't worry about the certificate. You'll have it by this afternoon.
B: Okay, thanks for your help.
A: You're welcome. Bye.

2 Point out to students that none of the options here are grammatically incorrect, but only one structure (*will* + infinitive) is appropriate for expressing an on-the-spot decision.

ANSWERS

I'll send you a copy of the certificate.
I'll deal with the email straight away.

3 Tell students to read the conversation, then complete the sentences with *will* + the infinitive of the verbs in the box. When students have completed the conversation, ask them to compare their answers with a partner, then read the conversation aloud in pairs to check that it makes sense.

4 **1.26** Play the recording for students to check their answers in 3.

ANSWERS

'll ring   'll send   'll send   'll write   'll fly

1.26

A: Have we got the details of the order from David Holmbrook?
B: No, but don't worry, I'll ring him now.
A: I tried – there's no answer.
B: Well, I'll send him an email, then.
A: You can't – our server is down.
B: Never mind – I'll send him a fax.
A: I don't think he has a fax machine.
B: Well, in that case, I'll write him a letter before I leave the office.
A: Oh, come on, that will take far too long.
B: So, we'll fly out to see him!
A: Oh, that's a bit expensive ...

5 Go through the instructions with the class. Explain that students work with a partner, presenting their problems then responding to their partner's problems by choosing the correct solution from their own chart. Before they begin, choose a student to work with and do one example for the class, e.g.

Student *I've got a problem. I've got a headache.*

You *Don't worry, I'll get you an aspirin.*

You *I've got a problem. I can't understand these figures.*

Student *Don't worry, I'll explain them to you.*

Students can find the answers on Student's Book page 146.

Take the role of either Speaker A or Speaker B and do the exercise with your student.

Language links

Direct students to the *Language links* section on page 43, for more information and practice exercises on *will* for on-the-spot decisions.

Language links

ANSWERS

Vocabulary

Business communication

1 a 8 b 2 c 5 d 4 e 1 f 7 g 6 h 3

2a

Dear Mr Gonzalez

Thank you for contacting Lexington Technical Support. Unfortunately, I do not understand the nature of the problem you are having, or, in fact, even the product you are using. Can you please write back with as much information as you can about what product you are using, what you are trying to do, what problem you are having, etc?

Best regards

Kamal Bouaissi

Technical Support Engineer

2b

Dear Richard Tennant

Thank you for registering your Lexington product. Your new customer number is 55563500. When calling Technical Support (925–253–3050) or Lexington Customer Service (800–225–4880), please have your customer number ready. We recommend writing your customer number in your Lexington manual, keeping it with our phone numbers and filing this email for future reference. Thank you for your interest in Lexington. If there is anything we can do for you, please let us know. We will be happy to help you.

Regards

Lexington Customer Service

3 *Across*

1	delivery	13	business	24	annoyed
6	prompt	15	correspondence	28	welcome
8	informal	19	check	29	down
9	handwriting	21	decision	30	confirm
10	fax	22	message		

Down

2	immediately	12	reply	20	that
3	expensive	14	Internet	23	skills
4	signature	16	worried	25	order
5	details	17	phoning	26	send
7	courier	18	mistake	27	cost
11	apologize				

Grammar

Practice 1

a 5 b 3 c 2 d 7 e 4 f 6 g 1

Practice 2

a I'll have coffee, please.

b I'll have salad for a starter.

c I'll pay for the drinks.

d I'll help you with your computer program.

e I'll take a taxi to the airport.

f I'll give you a lift home.

07 Hotels

In this first section, students discuss the frustrations that travellers sometimes experience with hotels, and study a series of conversations in which a traveller whose flight has been delayed tries to check into a hotel near the airport to wait for his connecting flight. Students then practise the conversation between the traveller and the hotel receptionist.

Warm-up

Ask students if they have any favourite hotels. If so, why do they like them? Do they think the standard of service in hotels is good, and is good service a factor for them when they are choosing where to stay?

1 Answer the questions as a class. When students have read and responded to the quotation in the left margin, you could have a class discussion on the best and worst hotels students have ever stayed in.

2 **1.27** Go through the questions with students before you play the recording so that they know what information to listen out for. You may need to pre-teach the expression *stretch my legs* (= walk, usually in order to alleviate stiffness after sitting for a long period of time), so that they can answer c. Tell them to cover the dialogue in 3 so that they do not simply read the script instead of listening. Play the recording. Check that students have understood that the airport employee offers to phone the hotel to see if they have any vacancies, but the traveller declines the offer because he prefers to walk to the hotel. It isn't far from the terminal building, and after his flight he is stiff and needs to stretch his legs.

ANSWERS

a At an airport
b He wants a recommendation for a hotel where he can sleep while he waits for his connecting flight.
c He is going to walk to the hotel to see if they have a room.

1.27

A: Hello. My connecting flight, IB621, was delayed so I've missed the flight to Caracas.
B: Yes, sir. I'm sorry about that. You're booked on the next flight.
A: Yes, but it's not until 11 tonight, right?
B: Yes. I'm afraid there's nothing before.
A: That's nearly eight hours to wait. Can you recommend a hotel I could try?
B: You could try the Travel Inn. It's not far from the terminal building.
A: Thanks. I really need somewhere to sleep.
B: Would you like me to phone for you, sir?
A: No, that's okay. I need to stretch my legs anyway. Thanks very much.

3 **1.27** Encourage students to complete as much of the dialogue as they can before comparing answers with a partner. Then play the recording again for them to check their answers.

ANSWERS

a was delayed, so I've missed
b booked on the next flight
c there's nothing before
d Can you recommend
e could try the Travel Inn
f like me to phone for you, sir

4 Have a class discussion on whether students have ever been in this situation and what they did. If no one has, ask them to say what they would do in the circumstances. You might like to suggest a few ideas, such as go into the city and do some sightseeing; take a shower and rest at the airport; find a computer terminal and do some work, etc.

5 **1.28** Again, go through the questions with students before you play the recording, so that they know what information to listen out for.

ANSWERS

a In a hotel (probably at the reception desk).
b He asks if he can pay for the room by the hour. No, he doesn't get what he wants.
c He would like a tomato and cheese sandwich and a sparkling water.
d Yes, it does.

1.28

A: Good afternoon.
B: Good afternoon. Do you have any rooms available?
A: Yes, sir. Is it just for tonight?
B: Yes. Well, actually I have a flight at 11 this evening so I'll check out in a few hours. I really need to get some sleep. Is it possible to pay for a room by the hour? I mean, do you have any reduced rates or anything?

A: Err … no, sir. I'm afraid not. I have to charge you for the whole night. I'm sorry, but that's the hotel policy.

B: Well, never mind. I'll take it anyway.

A: Okay, could I see your passport please? And I'll need a credit card.

B: Yes, of course. Here you are.

A: Would you like anything sent up to your room?

B: Yes, please. I'd like a tomato and cheese sandwich and a sparkling water. Oh, and I need to send some emails. Is there Internet access available?

A: Yes, of course. You can pick up the hotel Wi-Fi in every room. And I'll have the food sent up right away.

B: Right, thank you.

A: You're welcome. Have a good stay.

6 1.28 Students use the prompts to complete the questions. When they have finished and checked their work, play the recording again, pausing it at strategic points if necessary, in order to allow students time to check their answers and make any corrections.

ANSWERS

a Do you have any rooms available?
b Is it just for tonight?
c Is it possible to pay for a room by the hour?
d Could I see your passport?
e Would you like anything sent up to your room?
f Is there Internet access available?

7 Students work with a partner to act out the dialogue. If they cannot do this from memory using the prompts as reminders of what was said, allow them to refer to the listening script on page 150.

Time to kill

In this section, students read a text about a special kind of hotel that offers very small, but well-appointed and affordable rooms for travellers who have to spend hours waiting for planes at Gatwick Airport. These rooms can be booked for the night or for a four-hour slot. Students do some vocabulary work, identify true and false statements and use a diagram of the hotel rooms to find a mistake in the text. Students then use the article on the airport hotel to do some work on the formation of comparatives. They find examples of comparative sentences in the article and then make their own, comparing three different types of hotel. In a slightly freer exercise, they then compare three cities and three cars of their own choice.

Warm-up

Ask students to share experiences of any unusual hotels they have stayed in. What was unusual about them, and did they enjoy the experience?

1 When students have ticked the features they expect a good hotel to provide and added any ideas of their own, you could have a class discussion on what the most important features are (number them in order of importance), and ask students to say which ones would be a factor that would influence them if they were choosing a hotel.

2 Give students time to read the comments and discuss them with a partner. Encourage them to speculate on what the hotel is, where it is and what it might be like.

3 Ask students to read the comments again and find words and phrases to match those in the list. Find out how students 'kill time' when they are at airports.

ANSWERS

a had a few hours to kill
b reasonable
c short-hop flights
d stranded
e stretching out

4 Go through the statements with students before they read the article. Ask early finishers to note down reasons for their answers or to rewrite the false statements so that they are true. After checking answers, help students with any difficult vocabulary they may have encountered in the article.

ANSWERS

a false (They are more luxurious than standard three-star hotel rooms.)
b false (The rooms have sofas which convert to beds – you can sit on these.)
c false (The service is for travellers at airports.)
d false (None of the rooms has natural light, though the premium rooms have a window looking out onto a corridor.)
e true
f true
g false (The minimum stay is four hours.)
h false (He thinks they like having luxury facilities at an affordable price.)

5 Ask students to study the floor plan and the article carefully and identify the mistake.

ANSWER

The article says that each cabin has a sofa that converts into a double bed. The plan shows that this is only true of the Premium cabins; the Standard cabins have single beds.

6 Ask students to discuss with a partner whether they think they would like to stay in this hotel. Encourage them to think of reasons for their answer and to report back to the class. If you have any Japanese students, ask them if they have ever stayed in a capsule hotel and to tell the others about it if they have.

7 Focus attention on the example sentence and point out that the words *bigger than* are used to make a comparison between the size of two things. See if they can make a corresponding sentence comparing YOTEL rooms and Japanese capsules using the adjective *small* (*Japanese capsules are smaller than YOTEL rooms*). Point out the doubling of the consonant when *big* becomes *bigger*. Ask students to look back through the article on page 46 and underline any other sentences where things are compared. Write these up on the board and draw attention to the *more* + adjective + *than* construction used with longer adjectives, and the irregular form *better* (elicit that this is the comparative form of *good*).

They are also *more luxurious than* the average three-star hotel room.
Yotel aims for *better than* 200% occupancy.
... and finally, the afternoon guests looking for a *more comfortable place than* the airport terminal to have a siesta.

Language links

Direct students to the *Language links* section on pages 50–51 for more information and practice on comparative and superlative forms. The issue of spelling changes when comparatives and superlatives are formed is also addressed here.

8 Go through the instructions with the class, and form an example sentence on the board if necessary. This exercise could be done as a team game, with teams competing to make the largest number of comparative sentences. Accept any sentences that make sense and are grammatically correct.

9 Students work with a partner and compare three cities and three cars. As they work, go around helping with any adjectives they need, and making sure they are forming the comparatives correctly. Have a class feedback session to compare opinions.

Room service

In this section, students practise some of the language they are likely to need when staying in a hotel. First, they complete a dialogue between a hotel guest and room service, and then they make up their own dialogues using this as a model.

Warm-up
Focus attention on the title of this section and ask students what *room service* is. Has anyone ever used it? What did they ask for? Was the service good or bad?

1 **1.29** Ask students to try to complete the conversation before they listen to the recording. Then play the recording for them to check their answers.

a Could I have	b would you like
c Would you like	d 'll have
e will have it	f Anything else
g Good night	

🔘 **1.29**

A: Room service. My name is Johan. Can I help you?
B: Yes, this is room 301. Could I have an early morning call, please?
A: Certainly, sir. What time would you like the call?
B: At half past six.
A: 6.30. No problem. Would you like breakfast sent up to your room?
B: No, thanks. I'll have it in the dining room.
A: The dining room doesn't open for breakfast until 7.30.
B: Oh, in that case I will have it in my room. Just coffee and a croissant.

A: Coffee and a croissant. Anything else?
B: No, that's all.
A: Okay. Good night, sir.
B: Thank you. Good night.

Language links

Direct students to the *Language links* section on page 50 for more on the vocabulary of hotel services, and another example dialogue between a guest and room service for them to put in order.

2 Working with a partner, students change the phrases in bold then practise the new conversation together. Making minor changes to an existing conversation will prepare them for the next exercise, in which they have to devise their own conversations.

 Take the role of the guest and let your student be room service. Make changes to your orders and instructions so that your student has to listen carefully and respond appropriately. Then reverse roles and encourage your student to make changes. Be sure to respond correctly to whatever changes are made.

3 This exercise gives students the opportunity to put into practice some of the language they have learned in this unit. They can make the conversations as simple or as complicated as they wish, but make sure that they are giving enough detail. For example, Student B should say exactly what it is he/she would like to eat, rather than just ordering 'something to eat'. The room-service clerk in each conversation should ask questions to clarify exactly what is required. Make sure they swap roles.

World records

In this section, the focus is again on comparing hotels, but this time using superlatives. Students make sentences about several hotels which, for various reasons, are world-record breakers. They then do an information-gap activity to find out the prices of various hotels around the world, and talk about them using superlatives.

Warm-up
Go through the list of hotels in the table and ask students to raise their hands if they have stayed in any of them.

1 Go through the example sentence with the class and point out how the superlative is formed. Explain that we use comparatives to compare two things and superlatives to compare more than two. Refer to the *Language links* section on page 50 if necessary. Elicit a couple more sentences from the class to check that they can form superlative sentences correctly, then ask them to work individually to write sentences saying why each of the hotels in the list is a world-record holder. You may need to point out that you could use *highest* for both the Burj Al Arab and the Hotel Everest View (*highest* can refer to both height of building and its location), but *tallest* can only be used for the Burj Al Arab (*tallest* refers to height of building only).

The Palazzo Resort and Casino in Las Vegas, USA, is the largest hotel in the world. It has 8,108 rooms.
The Burj Al Arab in Dubai, UAE, is the tallest hotel in the world. It is 321 metres high.
The Royal Villa at Grand Resort Lagonissi in Athens, Greece, is the most expensive hotel in the world. A room costs $50,000 per night.
The Hotel Everest View in Nepal is the highest hotel in the world. It is 3,800 metres above sea level.
The Hoshi Ryokan in Awazu, Japan, is the oldest hotel in the world. It opened in 717.

2 Ask students to work with a partner to discuss whether they know of any new record-breaking hotels. Have a class feedback session to compare results.

3 Before putting students in pairs, focus attention on the example in the instructions. Students should then each look at their information and spend a few minutes deciding what they will need to say to their partners before they begin. Students can check their answers by comparing their completed charts.

Locating an office

In this section, students use the language they have learned for comparing things to make a choice between locations for a new European office. They discuss the options and think about the arguments in favour of each one.

Go through the instructions with students to make sure they understand the situation and what they have to do. Put them in pairs or small groups to discuss the various locations. Encourage them to use comparatives and superlatives to talk about the options and to make a final decision. For homework, you could ask students to write a report detailing the advantages and disadvantages of each location, and outlining their decision. Ask some students to read their reports to the class or collect them and display them on the wall for the others to read.

In company interviews Units 5–7
Encourage students to watch the interview and complete the worksheet.

Vocabulary
Hotel services
1 Room service. Katherine speaking. Can I help you?
Hello, Katherine. This is room 208 here. I'm feeling a bit hungry. I'd like to order a snack.
Yes, sir. What would you like?
Oh, I don't know. Perhaps a little smoked salmon?
Of course, that's no problem. Would you like it with some toast?
Yes, please. And I'd also like some mineral water.
Yes. Sparkling or still?
Oh, sparkling, please, and nicely chilled.
Right, sir. It will be with you in fifteen minutes.
Thank you, Katherine.
You're welcome, sir. Goodbye.
2 a affordable b deliver c comfortable d profitable
  e prefer f convert g expectations h operations

Grammar
Practice 1
a The post is slower than the Internet.
b Motels are cheaper than hotels.
c Mandarin is harder / more difficult to learn than English.
d Buses are more uncomfortable than trains.
e People think that accounting is more boring than marketing.
f Driving is more dangerous than flying.
g Large meetings are more inefficient than small ones.
h My last job was worse paid than this one.
i Four years ago, the economic situation was better than it is now.

Practice 2
a as b than c than d than e as

Practice 3
a It's not as difficult to build hotels in the USA as it is in Europe.
b A Chevrolet isn't as powerful as a Maserati GT.
c Turnover isn't as important as profitability.
d Sales are worse than last year.
e Yesterday was hotter than today.

Practice 4
Suggested answers
2002
a largest b larger than c most d smaller e larger
2012
a largest b lowest c as large as d fastest e largest

08 Telling stories

Learning objectives

This unit is about telling anecdotes or short stories about events, in your own experience, which are often funny or interesting and which may provoke someone else to reply with a story about a similar experience. As such, they are a useful way of maintaining a conversation and fostering good relationships between people.

Digital resources: Unit 8

Online Workbook; Extension worksheets; Glossary; Student's Book answer key; Student's Book listening script; Fast-track map

The unit starts with a recording of someone telling an anecdote about an incident that happened when he was a student. Students examine some of the language which is often used when telling stories and do some work on questions which they can use to encourage someone else to tell a story or give more details. They then work in pairs to tell anecdotes to each other.

Warm-up

Focus students' attention on the quotation from Sid Caesar at the top of the page. Ask them if they agree. Is it customary in their culture to respond to the telling of a story by telling one of your own? Do they enjoy listening to other people's stories or do they find it boring?

1 **1.30** Focus students' attention on the definition of *anecdote* in the margin and ask them what they think are the key features of a good story or anecdote (for example, a good punchline, a dramatic event). List these on the board and leave them up until students have completed 1. Tell students that they are going to listen to an anecdote and that they should first read the conversation and see if they can predict what the missing words are. Allow them to compare their answers with a partner or in small groups before playing the recording for them to check. Point out that the person telling the story first asks whether he has ever told the story to his friend before. The friend replies that he doesn't think he has. Ask students if they would say that they hadn't heard the story before, even if they had, just to be polite. Refer back to the list of features of a good anecdote that you put on the board and ask the students to say which of these are reflected in the story they have just heard.

ANSWERS

a ride   b was   c hitchhiking   d went   e police
f stopped   g important   h suppose

1.30
A: Look at that car!
B: Yes, very nice. It's a Porsche 911.

A: Did I ever tell you about the time I had a ride in a Porsche?
B: No, I don't think so.
A: It was when I was a student. I was hitchhiking in Europe and a man in a Porsche stopped. He took me all the way across Austria. We went about 220 kilometres an hour all the way.
B: What about the police?
A: Well, they stopped us about four times, but this chap just showed some identity card and they waved us on.
B: Was he someone important, then?
A: I don't know, I didn't ask. I suppose he was some sort of high-ranking official. Anyway, it was the fastest I've ever been in a car.

2 **1.31** Go through the example sentences with the class and point out that these two structures (*It was* + adverb and Past Continuous) are very common when people are telling stories. Their function is to set the scene and establish the background to a story. The structure *It was (when)* ... is immediately recognizable to native speakers of English as the beginning of a story, and they are likely to sit back and listen with enjoyment to what follows. Students make similar sentences using the prompts. Ensure that they realize that several alternatives are possible. Then play the recording for them to compare their answers. The material on the recording sets each sentence in a natural context and gives some idea of what the speaker is going to go on to say.

1.31
a   Yes, that was a long time ago. It was while I was living in Italy. I had this apartment in the centre of Milan ...
b   I can remember what happened. It was before I started working here. I was working on a temporary basis ...
c   No, it wasn't until much later. It was after I left university. I'd got my degree ...
d   Oh, yes, that reminds me. It was when I was working at ICL. I was in the marketing department ...
e   I had more time in those days. It was before I got married. In fact, I hadn't even met Mary ...
f   The timing was awful. It was just after my children were born. And there I was without ...
g   I'd just arrived in London. I was looking for a job. I bought the paper every day ...
h   Yes, I was still studying at the time. I was doing my Masters in the States. At the Harvard Business School, in fact ...
i   I was 19. I was studying at Cambridge. Things weren't going very well ...
j   No, it was with a different set-up. I was working for a small company north of here. One day the boss walked into ...
k   I was having a gap year after university. I was travelling through Asia. I'd just arrived in Ho Chi Minh City and ...
l   It happened last March. I was staying at the Continental Hotel in Prague. Lovely hotel, I recommend it.

3 **1.32** Elicit a couple of *Have you ever ...?* and *Did you ever ...?* questions from the class. Point out that these are useful structures for encouraging other people to tell you about their experiences. Ask students to match the questions with the answers. With weaker classes, do one or two as examples with the whole class before asking them to work individually. Play the recording for students to check their answers. You may need to point out that, as with the previous recording, the answers are set in a natural context with the speakers giving extra details to supplement their answers.

ANSWERS

a4   b1   c3   d8   e7   f2   g5   h6

 1.32

1

A: Did you ever hitchhike when you were a student?

B: Yes, but it was a long time ago, and I hated waiting in rain, so if I could, I took a train ...

2

A: Have you ever had a car accident?

B: No, I'm glad to say, but I nearly had one this morning! I pulled out and didn't see this motorbike. It was too close for comfort.

3

A: Have you ever been to Rome?

B: No, but I'd love to see the Coliseum one day. I once spent a few days in the north of Italy.

4

A: Have you ever lost any money on the stock exchange?

B: No and I've never made any either. I don't own any shares now.

5

A: Did you ever fail an exam at school?

B: Not at school, but I did at university. Actually I arrived late and they even didn't let me take it. It was a disaster.

6

A: Have you ever been camping?

B: Yes, lots of times. Actually we bought a camper van last year. We go somewhere most weekends.

7

A: Have you ever played a video game in 3D?

B: I didn't know you could. I've seen films with it though. I don't like having to wear those special glasses much.

8

A: Have you ever done anything illegal?

B: Not unless you count speeding and parking fines. Unless I've just forgotten something else!

4 The prompts here should enable students to come up with an anecdote to tell their partner, but you may need to give them plenty of time to prepare. This preparation could be done for homework. Focus attention on the *Useful language* box in the margin. As students tell their anecdotes, go around offering help and encouragement, and make a note of any interesting stories that could be repeated for the whole class. Encourage them to help each other by asking more questions, and praise any appropriate use of the phrases in the *Useful language* box.

 1:1 Let your student choose whether they want to be Speaker A or Speaker B, and make sure that you can supply an anecdote for either role in order to give them practice in being an active listener: listening to a story and asking questions to encourage you to say more/elicit more details.

B In my shoes

Learning objectives

This scenario is based on the topic of complaints and how to deal with them in a positive way.

Digital resources: Workplace Scenario B

 In company in action B1–B2 and worksheet; Extension worksheets; Glossary; Student's Book answer key; Student's Book listening script; Fast-track map

Warm-up

Ask students when they last made a complaint, either to someone within their own company or to someone in another company. Get them to say what the person did about their complaint and how satisfied they were with the result.

Focus attention on the definition of the phrase *in someone's shoes* and ask them how they think this is relevant to a unit about complaints. (To deal sensitively and successfully with a complaint, it can help to put ourselves in the person who's complaining's shoes – to think about how they must be feeling and how we would feel in their position.)

1 Students read the business advice and discuss the questions with a partner. Encourage them to report back to the class. Find out if they agree with the writer that complaints can be a positive thing.

1:1 Discuss the questions with your student and be prepared to contribute information about complaints that you have made or dealt with.

2 🎥 **B1** Go through the instructions and the questions with the class before you play the video, so that they know what the situation is. Then play the video and give them time to decide on their answers.

ANSWERS

a The new computer system isn't working properly and so she is unable to upload her report. She feels that she doesn't get enough support from the IT department.
b He first tries to avoid her, then denies that there is any problem with the system and then tells her he is too busy to help her.
c Students' own answers

🎥 B1
Part one

Vanessa: Claudia, I don't want to bother you, but can you upload your monthly report today, please?

Claudia: Can I just email it you?

V: Not really, I need it on the system for my meeting with Joe tomorrow. It's really important.

C: I know, the thing is I can't upload it. I had the report ready last week, but every time I try and add it to the system, nothing happens.

V: Well ask Eric to sort it out. I really need it done today, okay?

C: Okay! Coffee!

Part two

Claudia: Eric! ERIC! Have you got a minute? PLEASE!

Eric: What's the problem?

C: Thank you! Okay, the problem is I can't upload my monthly report onto the system.

E: I showed you how to do that last week. Go to the menu on the left, click Upload Manager, then click Add File and the rest is easy.

C: I know all that, but it doesn't work. Every time I select the file, nothing happens. I'm not happy with the new system at all; there are so many problems with it.

E: I know the new system had some problems at first, but everything is sorted out now.

C: Well, not for me! Could you just take a look at it for me, please?

E: Not now I'm afraid, I'm really busy at the moment.

C: Please, Eric; I need the report uploaded for Vanessa today.

E: And I need to get my work done for David. We're working on something really important.

C: This is urgent …

E: It's always urgent! Look, David said this project I'm doing now is the priority, so you'll have to wait, I'm afraid.

C: Put yourself in my shoes, Eric. Vanessa wants the report for her meeting with Joe tomorrow. She'll be really angry if it's not ready. And on a general point, I think we need to get more support from the IT department. Every time I come to you with a problem, you're too busy to help.

E: It's not my fault; David wants me to concentrate on this project. But I'll help you after that. Okay?

3 Focus attention on the advice given on page 55. Give students time to read it and consider their responses to the questions. Have a class feedback session about the issues raised.

ANSWERS
Students' own answers

4 Ask students to match the phrases in the box to the four steps outlined in the strategy. Check answers with the class, then elicit any more phrases they know for dealing with complaints and match these to the four steps, too.

ANSWERS

1 Can you describe the problem you had?
I'm really sorry to hear that you have had a problem. Can you tell me what happened?
Tell me what happened.

2 Are you referring to …?
Do you mean that …?
Have I understood that correctly?
So, you are saying that …

3 I can see there may have been a misunderstanding. Let me see what I can do.
I'll get back to you by the end of the week.
I'll look into this and get back to you as soon as possible.
The way you've described this, I can see why you are unhappy.

4 Could you give me your mobile number/email address so I can get back to you?
I'll get back to you by the end of the week.
I'll look into this and get back to you as soon as possible.

5 Read the instructions with the class and put students into pairs. Tell them to turn to their respective pages and follow the instructions. Students roleplay a conversation between Claudia and David McCann, in which David deals with Claudia's complaint according to the four-step strategy outlined in the text. As they do this, go around offering help and encouragement. Remind the students playing David to use the useful phrases for dealing with complaints in 4, and those playing Claudia to use the language given on page 135. Praise any use of these phrases. Take note of any particularly successful roleplays which could be performed for the whole class. Elicit how Claudia might feel after this conversation and compare it with how she probably felt after her conversation with Eric.

 Take the role of Claudia yourself, to allow your student to play David and practise dealing with a complaint according to the four-step strategy.

6 Ask students to individually complete the FEEDBACK: Self-assessment form on page 143 and then discuss answers with a partner. Ask students about anything they found surprising.

7 B2 Play the video and ask students to watch what happened when Claudia spoke to David. Allow time for them to respond to this and say how it was different from their roleplayed conversations. Then ask them to repeat the roleplay, changing roles.

 Get your student to repeat the roleplay (still playing David) and try to improve on their performance on the first time round.

B2

David: Come in, Claudia. Vanessa told me that there's something you want to talk to me about.

Claudia: That's right. I have a complaint and I hope you can help.

D: I'll do my best. Tell me what happened.

C: Well, it's about the new system the IT department installed. I still have problems with it, especially when I try uploading the monthly report.

D: Do you mean that the system isn't working properly?

C: Yes, there's something wrong with the Upload Manager.

D: That shouldn't be too serious. Talk to Eric, he can help you with that.

C: Well actually, that's what my complaint is about.

D: I see. Go on.

C: I asked for Eric's help, but he told me he was too busy.

D: Well, he is working on a very important project at the moment.

C: Yes, but it feels as though he's always too busy. To be honest, I don't feel we get the support we need from the IT department.

D: So, you're saying that you think they could help you more?

C: Yes. I know they're very busy, and I know that Eric has a lot of work to do at the moment, but look at it from my point of view; I need to upload my monthly report. If I don't, Vanessa can't update Joe about the marketing figures and they can't make a decision about next month. I know it seems like a small thing, but it's actually very important.

D: Yes, I understand, and the way you've described this, I can see why you're unhappy. I'll have a meeting with Eric and we'll try and rearrange his schedule so that he can make time to fix your problem.

C: I appreciate your help, but is there a way to make sure that it doesn't happen again?

D: I'll see what I can do. I agree with you, the IT department should be there to help anyone with a technical problem. We'll try to be more flexible in the future.

C: That would be great. Thanks so much.

D: No problem. I'll send you an email after my meeting with Eric. If there's anything else I can help you with, let me know.

D: Eric, it's David, have you got a minute?

8 Students work with a partner to think of three of their own situations where a complaint might be made, to use three of the examples given. Ask them to roleplay the conversations, taking turns to be the person who complains and the person who deals with the complaint. Go around offering help, and encouraging use of the four-step strategy and useful phrases.

Spirit of enterprise

Learning objectives

This unit is about successful businesses (enterprises) that have been built up by people who saw a gap in the market and worked hard to fill it. Three companies are focused on: an internet company supplying specialist car tyres, the successful Dreams bed company and Inditex, the Spanish fashion group, which has diversified within the fashion industry and made use of innovative and flexible management policies to develop and thrive within a competitive market.

The grammatical focus is on the Present Perfect versus the Past Simple, and the lexical focus is on word-building.

Digital resources: Unit 9

Online Workbook; Extension worksheets; Glossary; Phrase bank; Student's Book answer key; Student's Book listening script; Fast-track map

In this first section, students read about two people who successfully set up their own businesses. Working with a partner, they complete an information gap activity based on the texts, and then find examples of the use of the Present Perfect.

Warm-up

Focus attention on the quotation from Amancio Ortega at the top of the page. Explain that Ortega is the founder of the successful Inditex fashion group. Elicit some opinions about what the quotation means. (Suggested answer: To be successful in business, you need a vision for the future, not just an understanding of what works today.)

Tell students to discuss the question in the margin and ask who agrees that it is important to look ahead and think of the future.

1 Go through the instructions before putting students in pairs and telling them to read their assigned texts. As they complete their charts, go around offering help with any problems.

2 Ask students to take turns asking their partner questions and filling in the rest of their charts. With weaker classes, first elicit a couple of the questions they will need to ask, and write them on the board. Check answers with the class.

ANSWERS

	blackcircles.com	Dreams
First job of founder	He worked in a garage.	He worked in a furniture shop.
Age when he started the company	He was 20.	He was 35.
First business premises	An office with furniture rescued from a rubbish tip.	A small shop; in a bad state, but cheap.

Main product	High-performance specialist tyres.	Beds
Distribution network	Tyres ordered on the Internet and fitted at affiliated garages.	A fleet of over 100 vans
Customer services	The website encourages customers to give feedback on the service by emailing Welch directly.	Drivers wear special slippers so they don't make customers' homes dirty.
Recent developments	A joint venture partnership with Tesco, a leading retailer, and the launch of tesco-tyres.com, giving access to a massive nationwide customer base.	A move into the international market via franchising. Has launched its own YouTube channel and is on Facebook.

1:1 You could do the information-gap activity by reading one of the texts yourself. Alternatively, ask your student to read one of them before class and fill in the information for that text in the table. He / She can then read the other text in the lesson.

3 Give students time to read the text they didn't read before. Then ask them to underline the examples of the Present Perfect in both texts. Point out that the Present Perfect is often used to refer to past events (particularly recent events) where the time period is not specified and those which are part of an ongoing situation.

ANSWERS

blackcircles.com
blackcircles.com **has built up** a network of over 900 franchises. Since 2001, we **have supplied** and **fitted** tyres ... customers, many of whom **have bought** tyres from blackcircles.com again and again.
This joint venture **has meant** access to Tesco's massive nationwide customer base.
The company **has achieved** an estimate annual turnover of around £30 million.

Dreams
Dreams **has built** its business on four main selling points ...
Distribution **has been** the company's biggest challenge ...
Dreams **has** also **given** a lot of special attention to customer service.
The company **has grown** very quickly ...
It **has branched out** into the international market ...
It **has launched** a Dreams YouTube channel ...

Language links

Direct students to the *Language links* section on pages 61–62 for more information on the form and use of the Present Perfect, and practice exercises to help students use this tense correctly.

4 Read the definition of *entrepreneur* with the class and make sure everyone understands what it means. Remind them that they have just read texts about two entrepreneurs. Then ask them to read the extracts and think about their answers to the questions. Students work with a partner to discuss their thoughts and then report back to the class. When they are sharing information about famous entrepreneurs in their own country, ask them to give as much detail as possible about these people: what business they started, how old they were, how they did it, what people think of them, etc. Have a class vote on the opinion they agree with most.

 You could ask your student to do some research before class on one famous entrepreneur from his or her country.

5 **1.33** Make sure students understand that they are going to hear a radio programme in which there is a discussion about a book about entrepreneurs. Go through the questions with the class before you play the recording so that they know what information to listen out for.

ANSWERS

a The opinion in Wil Schroter's Blog.
b Two – Dreams and blackcircles.com.
c working for someone else before setting up a business, luck, taking risks, providing excellent customer service, setting up efficient distribution networks, hard work

1.33

A: ... next on today's programme we talk to David O'Brian about his new book on entrepreneurial success, *The Sky is the Limit*. So David, are entrepreneurs born or created?

B: Well, I think they're basically born, but obviously for an enterprise to be a success there are certain key business skills which have to be learned. Business studies courses provide an opportunity for the potential entrepreneur to get the skills without taking any risks while they do it. In other words, they can learn from the mistakes and experience of others.

A: So you don't think the classic MBA course does any harm?

B: No, not at all, but on the other hand an MBA is probably more important when you want to get a job working for someone else and not set up your own business.

A: Tell us about some of the people you feature in the book.

B: Well, Mike Clare, the founder of the bed shop chain, Dreams, and Michael Welch, the entrepreneur behind car tyre distributor, blackcircles.com, are both good examples of people who started work when they left school. They first picked up knowledge and skills while they worked for someone else, but each knew that his real mission in life was to be an entrepreneur – to set up a business, take risks and make a lot of money.

A: Apart from their first names, do they have anything else in common?

B: Well, Welch started his business when he was a lot younger, but actually they do have certain things in common. For example, both have made customer service a major selling point. This sounds obvious, but bad customer service is often the reason why businesses fail. Both businesses rely on efficient distribution and they've been successful at building up their networks.

A: Surely there is more to it than that?

B: Well yes, of course. They both saw an opportunity in a market where they felt they could do something better than the competition and had the confidence to take a risk. There is always a certain amount of luck involved, but the other thing I think they have in common is a capacity for hard work. They have worked incredibly hard to get where they are today.

6 **1.33** Give students time to read the gapped sentences and predict what words might be used to complete the phrases before you play the recording again.

ANSWERS

a started; left
b first picked up; worked; knew
c have made
d They've been
e have worked

7 Ask students to look at the completed sentences in 6 and answer the questions.

ANSWERS

- the Past Simple: a and b
- the Present Perfect: c, d and e
- an event or stage in life which is completely finished: a and b
- an achievement or event which is part of an ongoing situation: c, d and e

Change

In this section, the focus changes to another successful enterprise, this time in the fashion industry. Students begin by looking at ways to talk about change. They then listen to an extract from a radio programme about a successful Spanish company, and answer questions on this. Finally, they complete a report on changes in the company and then write one on a company they know.

Warm-up

Find out how many sayings or expressions students know which involve the word *change* or the concept of changing. Allow them to cite examples in their own language if they don't know any in English. You might like to teach them the sayings *A change is as good as a rest* and *A leopard can't change its spots*. Expressions they already know may include *changing room, a change for the better, change money/a battery/a tyre/one's clothes*, etc.

1 Focus attention on the three graphs and the words in the box. Ask students to identify which verbs go with which graphs (there are two for each graph). You could also elicit that *go up, not change* and *go down* are all more informal than *increase, fall* and *remain stable*.

A go up, increase
B remain stable, not change
C fall, go down

2 Before students start talking about what has happened in their country or region and company, go through the verbs in the box in 1 and elicit the Present Perfect forms (*has/have gone up*, etc). Then go through the examples with the class. Remind students that they don't have to restrict their discussion to the suggestions in 2 – they can talk about anything important which has happened recently. Working in groups, students make sentences about recent changes. Have a class feedback session for groups to report back on what they discussed.

3 **1.34** Go through the questions with the class and ask students to try to match the names and places in the box to their descriptions. Students then listen and check their answers. You may need to play the recording more than once to allow them to do this.

ANSWERS

a H&M   b Pablo Isla   c Zara   d La Coruña, Spain
e Arteixo, Spain   f Massimo Dutti   g Middle East

1.34

Inditex is a global fashion retailer with headquarters in Arteixo, Spain. It owns several retailers, including its flagship store, Zara. The multinational company has over 5,000 stores worldwide with 120,000 employees. The origins of Inditex go back to 1963 when Amancio Ortega Gaona started his career as a clothing manufacturer. Business was good for the young Spaniard, with several factories opening in the next decade. Finally, in 1975, the first Zara opened its doors in downtown La Coruña in Galicia, Spain.

From the start, Ortega wanted to make affordable and fashionable clothes, and this has remained at the core of Zara's business model. There are four key factors which are central to the company's business process and which have contributed to the huge success of this clothing chain. The first is turnover. In order to keep up with the latest fashions, Zara clothing has a very short shelf life. While competitors such as H&M and The Gap may be restricted to seasonal fashion trends, Zara's stock changes regularly in order to meet customer needs. With 60% of production taking place in Arteixo, that demand can be met quickly and efficiently.

The next two factors are variety and quantity, which are just as important as each other. The company makes small batches of each product which removes the expense of large storage warehouses and ensures that stock can be sold at full price – sales rarely

happen in Zara stores. Finally, Zara prides itself on communication with its end-users and has invested in an IT system which can track purchases from store to store and maintain contact with in-house managers who get feedback directly from the customer.

The customer remained central to Inditex's business philosophy throughout its expansion in the 1990s and 2000s. During this time it created and acquired additional retailers such as Pull & Bear, Massimo Dutti, Bershka, Stradivarius, Oysho, Zara Home and Uterqüe. Under the watchful eye of Ortega and current CEO Pablo Isla, Inditex's sales for 2012 were an astounding €13.79 billion. The only question now is, what next?

The obvious next step would be to continue with international expansion; regions such as the Middle East, Asia and South and North America are all potential growth markets for Inditex. However, what they gain in profit may be lost by high operating costs and increased competition, and the Inditex system and brand could become diluted. One option is to raise the company's online presence, which offers the freedom to expand without the financial burden.

One thing is for certain: Inditex is a company which is constantly moving forward, and always looking for new opportunities and ways to grow. It seems inevitable that the company will continue to expand and, with Zara leading the 'fast fashion' movement and appearing on more and more high streets across the world, Inditex will be a retail powerhouse long into the future.

4 **1.34** Go through the questions with the class before students listen and answer. You may need to play the recording more than once.

ANSWERS

a Over 5,000 stores and 120,000 employees
b Turnover, variety, quantity and communication
c To remove the expense of large storage warehouses and ensure that stock can be sold at full price.
d To track purchases from store to store and maintain contact with in-house managers, who get feedback directly from the customer.
e €13.79 billion
f Profit may be lost by high operating costs and increased competition, and the Inditex system and brand could become diluted.
g It offers the freedom to expand without the financial burden.
h Rapid stock turnover, which allows the stores to keep up with the latest trends in fashion.

5 Students work individually to match the sentence beginnings and endings. Check answers with the class.

ANSWERS

a 3 b 5 c 1 d 2 e 4

6 Students use the information in 3 and 4 to complete the report. Remind them of the use of the Present Perfect tense to show that events are part of a continuing process. Note that the answer to f can be *added* or *has added*; the Present Perfect can be used if the writer assumes that

Inditex are still adding stores. Ask one or two students to read their reports aloud. Check that the tenses have been used correctly.

ANSWERS

a opened   b La Coruña   c has grown   d 120,000
e has opened   f added/has added   g Massimo Dutti
h has given   i increased   j €13.79 billion

7 This writing exercise could be set for homework.

Language links

ANSWERS

Vocabulary

Word-building

Verb	Noun	Adjective
acquire	acquisition	acquired
reject	rejection	rejected
grow	growth	growing
succeed	success	successful
benefit	benefit	beneficial
innovate	innovation	innovative
flex	flexibility	flexible
operate	operation	operating
profit	profit	profitable
increase	increase	increased/increasing
fall	fall	fallen/falling
install	installation	installed

Grammar
Practice 1
a seen   b bought   c sold   d done   e found   f came
g put   h taken   i written   j broken   k set   l read
m fallen   n risen   o met   p thought

Practice 2
a I have lost my glasses.
b Prices have gone up by 3%.
c Economic growth has remained stable.
d Prices have fallen in the last five years.
e Molinex has sacked 2,000 workers.
f Mr Rodriguez has left the company.
g I have not seen John for a week.

Practice 3
a It's stopped raining.
b The photocopier has broken down.
c The taxi has arrived.
d The company has moved into the centre of town.
e You have lost your (presentation) notes.
f This is the third time you have given the same presentation.
g Philip Windish has changed companies.
h You have been very busy lately.

Practice 4
a 7   b 2   c 5   d 3   e 1   f 4   g 6

Practice 5
a have turned   b opened   c has added   d created
e acquired   f started   g launched   h have been
i has reached   j have increased   k finished

10

Stressed to the limit

Learning objectives

The focus of this unit is on stress and the effect it has on working people. It begins with a discussion of what things cause stress and presents an interview with four people talking about stress in their lives. Students then talk about which jobs they regard as most stressful and compare their opinions with some statistics. They then do some work on the use of *have to* to talk about what people's jobs entail. Avoidance and reduction of stress are the focus of a reading text which provides an opportunity for more work on word formation. Students then use *should* and *shouldn't* to talk about managers' and workers' responsibilities in the workplace. Finally, they do an extended roleplay activity concerning stress in the workplace and write a report on a company's problems in this area.

The grammatical focus is on *have to* and *should(n't)*, and the lexical focus is on stress at work.

Digital resources: Unit 10

Online Workbook; Extension worksheets; Glossary; Phrase bank; Student's Book answer key; Student's Book listening script; Fast-track map; Quick progress test 2; Mid-course test

---

In this first section, there is a discussion on the causes of stress and the factors in people's jobs which make one job more stressful than another. Students practise using *have to* to describe people's job responsibilities and *should* and *shouldn't* to talk about how people can reduce stress.

Warm-up

Focus attention on the quotation at the top of the page. Find out what students' attitude to pressure is. Is it a problem in their lives? Do they work well under pressure? Do they see it as a positive factor in increasing motivation and productivity at work? What is the most stressful thing they have ever had to do either at work or at home? How does their stress manifest itself? How do they cope with stress?

Language links ▶

Direct students to the **Phrase bank** in the **Language links** section on page 68 for useful expressions for talking about the effects of stress.

1 Make sure students understand the items in the box. Students work with a partner to list them in order of the amount of stress they produce. Have a class feedback session. Can students suggest any other factors?

2 **1.35–1.38** Go through the questions with the class before you play the recording, so that students know what information to listen out for. You may want to tell students

that not all of the questions are answered in interviews 3 and 4. After playing the recording, allow students to compare notes before checking the answers with the class.

ANSWERS

	Interview 1	Interview 2	Interview 3	Interview 4
a	Accountant	Shop assistant	Teacher	Self-employed architect
b	Yes	Yes, but at home, not at work	Yes	No
c	The speaker's boss, who is very demanding	Three children, a sick mother and a husband who doesn't help much	Working with teenagers	Mental attitude
d	Meeting deadlines	Looking after children	No	No

🔘 **1.35**

Interview 1

A: According to statistics, around 75% of all visits to the doctor are the result of work-related stress. Do you think you suffer from stress? That's the question we're asking in the streets of Edinburgh. Excuse me, I'm from the radio programme *Work Today*. We're doing a survey on stress. Would you mind answering some questions?

B: Eh, well, actually, I'm in a bit of a hurry, but ... erm ... go on, then.

A: Thank you. What's your job?

B: I'm an accountant.

A: Do you suffer from stress in your work?

B: Eh, yes, I do, I think.

A: What symptoms do you notice?

B: Erm, I get a lot of headaches and I sleep very badly.

A: And what causes your stress?

B: It's my boss. He's a real ... well, let's just say he doesn't exactly make life easy. He always wants things done for yesterday.

A: Thank you very much.

🔘 **1.36**

Interview 2

A: ... and what do you do?

C: I work in a shop.

A: Do you suffer from stress?

C: No, not at work, I don't. I find being at home more stressful.

A: Why's that?

C: Well, I've got three children, and my mother's ill. She lives with us. And my husband ... well, he doesn't help much.

A: And do you have any physical symptoms?

C: Well, I get a bit on edge at times and then I get this horrible rash on my neck.

A: So, stress is a problem in your life.

C: Yes, definitely.

 1.37

Interview 3

A: ... and you, sir. Do you suffer from stress?

D: Well, to tell the truth, I'm off work at the moment because of it.

A: Really, what do you do?

D: I'm a teacher. I work with teenagers and I don't know why, but every year, they seem to get worse.

A: Yes, that does sound stressful.

D: Everyone thinks teaching's an easy option because of the holidays, but you get to a point where you just can't handle it any longer. You lose control.

A: Well, I hope things get better for you.

D: Thanks, but I think that basically the solution is probably to change jobs. Fortunately, I'm still young enough to do that.

A: Right. Good luck, then.

 1.38

Interview 4

A: Can I ask you if you suffer from stress?

E: Who? Me? No, not at all. I don't really understand what it is, really.

A: And what do you do for a living?

E: I'm a self-employed architect. I work for myself.

A: I see, and what's your secret?

E: I'm sorry?

A: I mean, how do you avoid getting stressed?

E: I think it's all down to a philosophy of life. I just take each day as it comes. I don't worry about things. What I say is that if you've got a problem, solve it. And if you can't because there's no solution, there's no point in worrying, because that won't help.

A: So, you think avoiding stress is to do with mental attitude, not what you do?

E: Yes, that's basically it.

A: Well, thanks very much.

E: Not at all.

3 Have a class discussion to find out how many students agree with the last speaker.

4 Ask students to work in small groups to discuss and decide on an order for the jobs. Tell them to give reasons why they think one particular job is more stressful than another. Encourage them to use *have to* to talk about what each job entails. Have a class feedback session before students turn to page 132 and compare their answers with the statistics there. Elicit students' reactions to the information.

5 Make sure that students know that *doesn't have to* means that something is not necessary. It is not a prohibition and doesn't mean the same as *mustn't* or *shouldn't*. Early finishers can compare the other jobs in

4 or construct similar sets of prompts for other students to compare aspects of jobs from 4. Ask several students to read out their sentences and ask the others if they agree with them.

a An air traffic controller has to take decisions very quickly. A factory worker doesn't have to be creative.

b A lawyer has to wear a suit. A secretary has to type letters. A lawyer doesn't have to type letters.

c Middle managers have to solve day-to-day problems. Chief executives have to take strategic decisions.

d A shop assistant has to deal with the public. A computer programmer has to know computer languages.

e A lorry driver has to drive long distances. A taxi driver has to memorize street maps.

f A nurse has to work at night. A factory worker has to wear special clothes.

g An accountant has to be honest. A telephonist doesn't have to use a computer.

h A teacher has to tell people what to do. An engineer doesn't have to wear a tie.

Language links

Direct students to the *Language links* section on pages 68–69, for more information and practice exercises on the use of **have to** and **don't have to**.

6 Students work with a partner, taking turns to interview each other about the responsibilities of their own jobs. They could use some of the prompts from 5 if they are stuck for ideas on things to ask. When they have finished, ask them to change partners and tell their new partner about their original partner's job.

7 Students match words which will appear in the article on the next page to their definitions. This will help them when they come to read the text. Allow students to compare their answers with a partner before checking answers with the class.

ANSWERS

a 4 b 3 c 1 d 5 e 6 f 2 g 7

Language links

Direct students to the *Language links* section on page 68, for more useful vocabulary connected with stress at work.

8 You could have a class vote on whether the sentences are true or false. Encourage students with strong opinions to give reasons for their answers.

9 Ask students to read the article quickly to find out if the writer agrees with their conclusions in 8. Ask students to read the article again more carefully and elicit their reactions to it. Does anything in the article surprise them? Do they agree or disagree with any of it?

The writer appears to think that a, d and e are false, and that b and c are true.

It isn't clear whether the writer thinks it's easy for companies to reduce stress or not (e), but certainly believes it is beneficial to do so.

10 Go through the question and do an example for the class if necessary. Tell students to compare their answers with a partner, then check answers with the class. Encourage students to use charts like this whenever they record new vocabulary in their notebooks. Knowledge of a word is greatly enhanced if you also know other forms of it and can use them all correctly.

noun	verb	adjective
stress	stress	stressful
motivation	motivate	motivated
creativity	create	creative
excitement	excite	exciting

11 This exercise consolidates the learning in 10 by putting the new words into a context. Check the answers by asking various students to read the sentences aloud, so that they hear them used in context.

a stressful   b motivated   c creativity   d exciting

12 Students work individually to write sentences about their own company and then show them to a partner. Their partners should ask for more information, where appropriate.

13 Read the example sentences with the class and elicit further sentences using *should* and *shouldn't*. Allow students to compare their answers to the exercise with a partner before checking answers with the class.

a To work well, you should have a certain amount of pressure.
b Companies should try to reduce the level of stress.
c Workers shouldn't work very long hours.
d Managers should communicate ideas.
e Companies should invest money to improve conditions.
f Managers should learn to motivate workers.
g Workers should have time to rest.

Language links

Direct students to the *Language links* section on pages 68–69, for more information and practice exercises on the form and use of *should* and *shouldn't*.

14 This exercise could be set for homework. Ask students to bring their sentences to the next lesson and report back to the class about what they think their company should and shouldn't do.

The consultant's report

In this section, students continue their examination of stress in the workplace and work together to create and write a report on a company which has problems with stress management.

You will have to make up a company and play the role of the stressed employee. Your student can interview you in the role of management consultant and then write a report on the interview.

Read the instructions step by step with the class and make sure students understand what they have to do at each stage. Monitor the stages carefully, giving help and encouragement where necessary. Set a time limit for each stage and don't allow students to move on to the next stage until the whole class is ready, otherwise you may have some students rushing through to the end when some students are still working on step 2. You could display the finished reports on the wall to allow everyone in the class to read them.

Language links

Vocabulary

Stress at work

1 a stressful   b lawyer   c responsibilities   d motivating
  e employer   f illness   g communication   h training
  i unnecessary   j recognize   k relations/relationships
  l creative   m management   n performance

2 a Do you find your work **stressful**?
  b My boss doesn't make life **easy**.
  c My husband doesn't **help much**.
  d At times I get a bit on **edge**.
  e 75% of visits to the doctor are the **result** of stress.
  f Everyone thinks that teaching is an **easy option**.
  g I hope things get **better** for you.
  h There's **no point** in worrying about things.
  i I work for **myself**.

Grammar

Practice 1

a have to sign   b don't have to wear
c have to finish   d has to get up
e have to go   f don't have to do
g have to make   h don't have to come
i have to get   j have to show
k doesn't have to work

Practice 2

a Do I have to finish this today?
b Do you have to dress formally for work?
c How many times do you have to go abroad a year? / How many
  times a year do you have to go abroad?
d When do we have to complete the order?
e Do we have to go to English classes this year?
f Do you have to drive much in your job?

Practice 3

a You should go
b You should go
c You shouldn't spend
d You should leave
e You should have
f You shouldn't work
g You should set up

Practice 4

a have to/should
b shouldn't
c should/have to
d shouldn't; should/have to
e have to
f have to
g should
h shouldn't
i should
j don't have to

11 Top jobs

In this first section, students are presented with an account of the activities of the media executive Dan Gibson, which is then used to teach the use of the Present Perfect for talking about the unfinished past and time expressions with *for* and *since*.

Warm-up

Focus attention on the quotation at the top of the page. Ask students whether they agree that in business good leaders are more important than good managers. Ask them to work with a partner to come up with suggestions for five skills needed to be a good leader. Pool results on the board and then have a class vote to choose the top five.

1 Go through the questions with the class to make sure everyone understands them. Then students work with a partner to discuss their answers. Have a class feedback session to compare ideas. Make sure students do some analysis, giving reasons for how the Internet has changed the world of media.

ANSWER
Students' own answers

2 Go through the questions with the class so they know what information to look for as they read the article extract.

ANSWERS
a LA.
b He wasn't very good at it and only got a few acting jobs.
c No, he says it worked out in the end.
d Students' own answers

3 Focus attention on the profile of Dan Gibson on page 71. Ask students to complete the sentences using this information and the verbs in the box.

ANSWERS
a started working   b has worked
c still works   d joined
e has been   f is not

4 Students match the sentences in 3 to the verb forms. Check answers with the class. Point out or elicit that there are two groups of three sentences in 3. In each group there are two sentences about the past and one about the present. Elicit that we use the Past Simple for actions in the past that are now completed; the Present Perfect for the unfinished past, to talk about when present situations began or how long they have continued; and the Present Simple for present situations. Point out the use of *since* in sentence e to talk about a point in time (*since 2000*) and *for* in sentence b to talk about a period of time (*for over 20 years*).

ANSWERS
Past Simple: a, d
Present Simple: c, f
Present Perfect: b, e

5 Allow students to compare their answers with a partner before checking answers with the class. Check the answers by reading out the words in the box and telling students to put up their right hand if the word goes with *since* and their left hand if it goes with *for*.

ANSWERS
since: 1945, 5 o'clock, he arrived, I was born, last year, this morning, yesterday
for: 20 years, a couple of days, a few years, a long time, five minutes, months

▶ Language links

Direct students to the *Language links* section on pages 74–75, for more information about the use of the Present Perfect, and practice exercises to help them use this tense correctly.

6 Students write six sentences in the Present Perfect, using *for* and *since*, which are true for them. Ask them to show their sentences to a partner and check that the Present Perfect, *for* and *since* are used correctly. You might like to ask various students to read out their sentences to the class.

7 Do part a) with the class. Ask which question is about an action in the past which is now completed (*Why did you choose it?*), and elicit that this requires the Past Simple. Then ask which question is about a present situation (*What kind of car do you have?*) and elicit that this requires the Present Simple. Finally, ask which question is about a situation that began in the past, but is still continuing (*How long have you had it?*). Elicit that this requires the

Present Perfect. Then ask students to form questions with the remaining prompts. Parts f) and g) give students more flexibility to form their own questions about subjects which interest them. Finally, check answers with the class.

ANSWERS

a What kind of car do you have? How long have you had it? Why did you choose it?

b Do you have a mobile phone? How long have you had it? Do you use it a lot?

c Where do you live? How long have you lived there?

d Who do you work for? How long have you worked there? What is your job?

e How long have you had your present job? Do you like it?

f Students' own questions

g Students' own questions

8 Students work with a partner, taking turns asking and answering the questions in 7. Make sure the questioner tries to get more information each time by asking follow-up questions.

9 Students work with a different partner, sharing the information they learned about their previous partner.

 1:1 Ask your student to answer the questions for a colleague or friend, and then tell you about that person.

Entrepreneur of the year

In this section, students continue to work on the Present Perfect and look at the difference between it and the Present Simple and Past Simple. The focus is on a radio programme about the founder of an online auction site who was named as World Entrepreneur of the Year 'Ernst and Young' in 2012. Students correct the differences between the written and spoken accounts, do some work on some of the useful vocabulary in the article and use it to complete sentences.

Warm-up

Find out if your students have experience of buying and selling things through online auction sites, such as eBay™. Ask them to talk about the advantages and disadvantages of using such sites.

1 2.01 Focus attention on the words and phrases students have to listen out for. The recording is quite long, so reassure them that all they have to do is to number the items in the order they hear them. You could ask students to put their hands up as soon as they hear an item. In this way, weaker students will be helped by stronger students alerting them to the fact that one of the target items has just been mentioned.

ANSWERS

1 online auction site	2 Stanford
3 John Muse	4 online commerce platform
5 Latin American eBay™	6 mobile devices
7 1.2 million transactions	

2.01

In July 2012, Marcos Galperin, founder and CEO of MercadoLibre, was named as an 'Ernst and Young World Entrepreneur of the Year'. His company is the world's second-largest online auction site. Since September 2001, it has been a partner company of the US auctioneer, eBay™, which acquired 19.5% of MercadoLibre in exchange for its Brazilian subsidiary, Ibazar.com.br.

Galperin grew up in Buenos Aires, but went to college in the United States. After graduating, he returned home and worked for three and a half years at the largest oil company in Argentina. He then went back to the United States to do an MBA at Stanford. While Galperin was there, he pitched his ideas for an Internet company to John Muse, the founder of a private equity fund. Muse thought the ideas showed potential and agreed to invest.

Galperin has known the co-founder of MercadoLibre, Hernan Kazar, since they were students together at Stanford. In fact, after creating the business plan and securing financing, Galperin recruited several classmates there to help manage the business. Since its creation in 1999, MercadoLibre has grown dramatically to become the largest online commerce platform in Latin America, with sites across nine countries, including Brazil, Argentina and Mexico.

Back in the 1990s there were many start-up companies trying to become the Latin American eBay. Galperin was different to the others in that he focused more on IT and the platform and less on marketing or PR. As a result, his company flourished while the rest went bankrupt. Following the rise of smartphones and tablet computers, it modified its original technology so it could run its services on mobile devices and allow external developers to build applications.

Company sales grew 37% between 2007 and 2011, and MercadoLibre is the eighth highest-ranked retail site for traffic in the world. During 2011, there were almost 53 million products sold, an increase of 35% from 2010. Every month the company manages more than 1.2 million transactions, attracting 750,000 buyers, and business has more than doubled every year for the last five years.

2 2.01 Make sure students realize that there are eight mistakes in the article, not the radio programme, and that these are factual rather than grammatical errors. Ask them to read the article carefully and underline any information that they think is different from what they heard in 1. Allow them to compare notes in pairs or small groups before playing the recording again for them to check, or asking them to turn to page 152 to check the script against the article.

1 Galperin's company is the second largest online auction site, not the largest.
2 eBay™ acquired 19.5% of MercadoLibre, not 5%.
3 Galperin worked at the largest oil company in Argentina, not the largest gas company.
4 Galperin recruited classmates, not teachers, to help manage the business.
5 MercadoLibre is the largest online commerce platform in Latin America, not in North America.
6 He focused more on the platform, not on getting investment.
7 MercadoLibre is the eighth highest-ranked retail site for traffic in the world, not the tenth.
8 Every month MercadoLibre attracts 750,000 buyers, not 75,000.

3 Allow students to do this with a partner if they wish. Then check answers with the class.

ANSWERS

Since September 2001, it has been a partner company of the US auctioneer, eBay, ...
Galperin has known the co-founder of MercadoLibre, Hernan Kazar, since they were students ...
Since its creation in 1999, MercadoLibre has grown dramatically ...
... business has more than doubled every year for the last five years.

4 Tell students to cover the article in 2 as they try to reconstruct the story from the words in 1. Alternatively, ask students, in pairs, to reconstruct half of the story each. The student who is not speaking can look at the article and give help by prompting if his / her partner gets stuck.

5 Allow students to work with a partner to find the words and phrases. You could make this a race between pairs to see who can find them all first. The winning pair should read out their answers and the others should fill in any gaps they have.

ANSWERS

a entrepreneur	b subsidiary
c to go to college	d to pitch
e business plan	f to go bankrupt
g retail site	

6 Students use the words and phrases they have just learned to complete the sentences. Remind them that they may have to modify them to make them fit the sentences. Check answers by asking students to read their sentences aloud so that they hear the words in context.

ANSWERS

a entrepreneur	b go bankrupt
c pitching	d business plan
e on retail sites	f go to college
g subsidiary	

7 As students write their own sentences, go around checking that they are using the words and phrases correctly.

Language links

Direct students to the *Language links* section on page 74, where they will find more on the vocabulary of company news.

Headhunters

In this section, students look at the practice of tempting top executives to move jobs by promising them a better salary or a better position. This is done by professional companies called 'headhunters' who act on behalf of a client who is looking for someone to fill a vacant post. Headhunters discreetly contact suitably-qualified people who may be interested in moving jobs and applying for this post. Students listen to a phone call from a headhunter, answer questions about what is said and then discuss whether they think it is an ethical way to behave. They then interview each other about their present jobs and write short texts which would be useful to a headhunter.

Warm-up

Focus attention on the definition of *headhunter* in the margin. Tell students that the word *headhunter* originally referred to a member of a primitive tribe who cut off enemies' heads as battle trophies. Ask them if they think these two types of headhunter have anything in common. (Perhaps a degree of ruthlessness, a lack of concern for the target, a determination to succeed ...)

1 🔘 **2.02** Focus attention on the photo. Find out if students work in open-plan offices where everyone can hear everybody else's phone calls. What are the advantages of this? What problems can it create? What do they do if they receive a personal phone call at work? Go through the questions before you play the recording so that students know what information to listen out for. Allow them to compare their answers with a partner or in small groups, then check answers with the class or play the recording again.

ANSWERS

a He wants to headhunt him for a job.
b About six years ago
c He worked for Navigate as a trainee manager.
d A year
e About two years ago
f Yes, he has recently become a father.
g Not at first, but he does agree to think about it and talk to him again.

🔘 **2.02**

A: Good morning. Could I speak to Peter Davis, please?
B: Speaking.
A: Oh, hello, Mr Davis. My name is John Lindsay.
P: What can I do for you, Mr Lindsay?
B: It's more a case of what I can do for you ... Erm, how long have you worked for Blueprint International, Mr Davis?
A: For about six years. Why do you ask?
B: And before that you worked for Navigate for three years?
A: Yes, I joined them as a trainee manager when I left university. But ... what is this about?
B: And you were made head of the International Division a year ago. How's it going?

A: Very well, thank you. Now, could you tell me what you want, Mr Lindsay?

B: I'd like to talk to you about an extremely interesting career opportunity. I work for *People Search*, the management consultants. We've been approached by a client who's looking for someone with just your professional profile.

A: Oh, I see. So that's what it's about. Listen, Mr Lindsay, I'm really quite busy and ...

B: Yes, I understand that, but you should know I'm talking about a considerable salary increase. You've been married for a couple of years now and recently became a father, I believe.

A: What's that got to do with it?

B: Well, think about your family and the financial possibilities of an advantageous career move at this moment in your life. I think you should at least talk to me.

A: Erm, well, I suppose so. What's the name of the company?

B: I'd rather not say over the phone. Perhaps we could meet to discuss things further?

A: I'm not sure I'm that interested ... Blueprint International have been very good to me.

B: Oh, come on, Peter! What are the real prospects in your present post? You've got as far as you can in Blueprint. Do you want to be in the same place ten years from now? At least find the time to talk to us.

A: I'd like to think about it. Can I phone you back?

B: No, I'd prefer to phone you back myself in a couple of days. In the meantime, think about what I've said. A more stimulating work situation, not to mention a considerable rise in salary ... Talk it over with your wife.

A: Fair enough.

B: Oh, and one more thing, Peter. I'd appreciate it if you didn't mention this call to anyone in your company, okay?

A: Yes, yes, all right. So, you'll call me, then?

B: That's right. In a couple of days. We'll arrange a meeting somewhere. Bye for now, then.

A: Bye.

2 Students work with a partner to discuss the questions. Ask them to tell each other if they have any personal experience of being contacted by a headhunter. What was their reaction? Does anyone hold their present position because they were headhunted? Have a class feedback session to compare opinions.

ANSWERS

Students' own answers

3 Students read the report individually.

4 Students work with a partner, asking each other questions to write a similar report to the one in 3. Go around giving help where necessary, ensuring students are using the phrases in the box and forming questions in the Present Perfect correctly. The writing of the report could be set for homework if students do the preparatory interviews in class.

 1:1 Ask your student to interview you and make notes on your answers. Then set the writing of the report for homework and go over it in the next lesson.

In company interviews Units 9–11
Encourage students to watch the interview and complete the worksheet.

Language links

ANSWERS

Vocabulary
Company news
a 4 b 10 c 8 d 1 e 7 f 5 g 9 h 2 i 3 j 6

Grammar
Practice 1
a since b since c since d for e for f since
g for h since i Since j for

Practice 2
a How long have you worked here?
b How long has he known about this problem?
c How long has she been a director of the company?
d How long have you wanted to change jobs?
e How long have they had their website?
f How long has he been interested in working for us?
g How long has he had a company car?
h How long has she been responsible for that account?

Practice 3
a He's worked here since January.
b He's lived in Paris since he was born.
c He's been a computer programmer since he left university.
d They've made furniture for over a hundred years.
e She's owned a business for five years.
f They've been market leaders since 1998.

Practice 4
a I've known him since university.
b Mr Jones has been here for hours.
c How long have you had your car?
d I've been in this job since January.
e I've known about the problem since yesterday.
f They've been divorced for two years.

Practice 5
a He's been an aeronautical engineer since 1990.
b He has run marathons since 1984.
c He studied engineering at university for three years / from 1986 to 1989.
d He has been interested in boats since 1991.
e He has been married since 1992.
f He worked for Rolls Royce for five years / from 1990 to 1995.
g He has had a yacht since 1993.
h He lived in Canada for six years / from 1995 to 2001.
i He has lived in the UK since 2001.
j He has had a job in Portsmouth since 2006.
k He has worked for P & W since 1995.
l He has run ten marathons since 1984.

12 Conversation gambits

Learning objectives

In this unit, students learn some useful language and tips for starting up, continuing and ending conversations with strangers. Business people travelling on their own can feel isolated if they don't have anyone to talk to, and a casual conversation at the conference bar has often led to a good business contact and even increased business for a company.

The unit begins with a list of strategies for starting up conversations with people you don't know. Students then listen to and complete some conversations between strangers at a conference and learn some more good ways of initiating a conversation. They then discuss suitable and unsuitable topics of conversation and polite ways to end a conversation.

Digital resources: Unit 12

Online Workbook; Extension worksheets; Glossary; Student's Book answer key; Student's Book listening script; Fast-track map

Warm-up

Focus students' attention on the general definition of *gambit* in the margin. Ask students what they think *gambit* means in the expression *conversation gambit* (a technique for getting someone to have a conversation with you). Elicit suggestions as to why enticing someone into a conversation with you could be advantageous to you in different situations, business-related and personal.

Focus attention on the quotation from George Bernard Shaw at the top of the page and ask students if they agree with it. What kind of things do most people want to know about other people?

1 Focus attention on the photo and ask students where they think this is and who they think the people are. Then give them time to read the list of strategies thoroughly and think about which ones they might use at a conference. When they have discussed these strategies with a partner, ask them to report back to the class on their opinions and find out which are the most and least popular ideas.

2 **2.03–2.06** Make sure that everyone understands that they are going to hear four conversations at a conference. Discourage stronger students from reading the gapped conversations in 3 (if they notice that these are the same), but with weaker students, you might like to get them to read along as extra support. Ask students to identify the strategies from 1 that the speakers use.

ANSWERS
1 b 2 d 3 b/d 4 b/e

2.03

Conversation 1

A: Excuse me, are you here for the ITM conference?
B: Yes, that's right.
A: Me too. Do you know where to register?
B: I think it's over there.
A: Oh, yes. Right, I'm Paulo, by the way.
B: Hello, Paulo, I'm Kate. Let's go and register.

2.04

Conversation 2

A: Phew! Is it me, or is it boiling in here?
B: Yes, they always seem to have the heating on full.
A: So, it's not your first time?
B: No, it's my fourth time here.
A: Oh, right, so you're an old hand. I'm Boris.
B: David. Pleased to meet you.

2.05

Conversation 3

A: Is it my mobile phone, or is there some problem with coverage here?
B: Oh, hang on. No, mine seems to be working okay.
A: Typical, flat batteries and nowhere to charge up.
B: Can I lend you mine?
A: Oh, that's very kind, but I was expecting a call on this number.
B: I see.
A: My name's Nadine, by the way. From Xanadu Electronics.
B: Pleased to meet you. I'm Miko.

2.06

Conversation 4

A: Excuse me, do you know anything about this speaker?
B: No, I'm sorry, I don't.
A: I can't find my programme notes.
B: Oh, here. Borrow mine.
A: Thanks. By the way, I'm Bill Smart from Silicon Technologies.
B: Right, how do you do? I'm Kazuo Yamada from Lexico.

3 **2.03–2.06** Stronger students could be asked to see if they remember enough to complete the gaps before you play the recording for a second time. When students have completed the conversations and listened again to check their answers, they could practise them with a partner. All the conversations end with the people introducing themselves, but they each start with a slightly different conversation gambit. Ask students to describe precisely what these are (1 asking about where to register for the conference; 2 commenting on the temperature of the conference hall; 3 mentioning a problem with mobile phone coverage and asking if the other person has it too; 4 asking if someone knows anything about the speaker at a conference). You could ask students to take each of these conversation gambits and suggest another opening line for each. Ask students whether they think the conversations would have been equally successful if the first speaker in each case had simply walked up to the other person and said 'Hi, I'm ...'.

ANSWERS

1 Excuse me, **are you here for** the ITM conference?
  Me too. **Do you know where to register**?
  I'm Paulo, **by the way**.
  Hello, Paulo, I'm Kate. **Let's go and register**.
2 Phew! Is it me, or **is it boiling in here**?
  So, it's not **your first time**?
  Oh, right, so **you're an old hand**.
  David. **Pleased to meet you**.
3 Is it **my mobile phone**, or is there some problem with coverage here?
  Oh, **hang on**. No, mine seems **to be working** okay.
  Can I lend you mine?
  Oh, **that's very kind**, but I was expecting a call on this number.
  My name's Nadine, by the way.
4 Excuse me, do you know **anything about this speaker**?
  I can't find **my programme notes**.
  Oh, here. **Borrow mine**.
  Right, **how do you do**?

4 Students have now learned several ways to start up a conversation. The focus now turns to what they can talk about once the introductions are over. Ask students to discuss with a partner which topics in the box they think are 'safe' to discuss with people you don't know very well, and which ones they think you should avoid. Have a class feedback session to compare opinions.

ANSWERS

Answers will depend on cultural differences, but the safest topics are probably art, business, cars, local attractions, music, the stock exchange and the weather.

5 **2.07** Read the instructions and the questions with the class before playing the recording. Ask students to answer the questions.

ANSWERS

a He asks if he can look at the other man's newspaper.
b He introduces the topic of football.

 2.07
A: Excuse me. Would you mind if I had a quick look at your newspaper?
B: Er, no, go ahead. I've finished with it.
A: There's just something I want to check out.
B: No problem. Take your time.
A: Thanks. By the way, my name's Allan.
B: Nice to meet you.
A: Here's your paper then. Thanks very much.
B: Don't mention it.

A: I'm glad to say we won.
B: Sorry?
A: The football results.
B: Oh, I see.
A: I think I'll have a coffee. Can I get you something? If you don't have anything else to do, that is.
B: I was just about to go, actually, but ... yes, why not, ... Al, I think you said your name was?
A: Allan, Allan Vilkas.

6 Read through the instructions and the headlines with the class and ask students to work with a partner, taking turns pretending to return a newspaper and start a conversation about one of the headlines. Encourage them to maintain their conversations for as long as possible. You might like to point out that in the conversation Allan had in 5, he didn't get a very encouraging response when he introduced the topic of football (*Oh, I see*). You could ask students what they think the other man could have said to keep the football conversation going.

7 These are useful questions for students to learn, which they will be able to use in a variety of situations. After students have formed the questions and matched them to the answers, check answers by having one student ask the question and another provide the answer, so that the class hear the language used in a natural context.

ANSWERS

a Where are you from? 1, 7
b How long have you been here? 5, 9
c How long are you staying? 2, 3
d What do you think of Belfast? 4, 8
e Are you here on business? 6, 10

8 **2.08** Explain that students are about to hear the second half of the conversation that they heard in 5. Play the recording. Students listen and circle the questions and answers that they hear. Check answers with the class.

ANSWERS

Questions: a, d, e, c   Answers: 4

 2.08
B: I'm Sean, Sean O'Malley.
A: Pleased to meet you, Sean. Can I get you something?
B: A coffee, please.
A: Right. Two coffees, please.
C: Right, sir.
B: So, Allan, where are you from?
A: Well, I was born in Lithuania, but I've lived in Germany most of my life. Are you from here?
B: Yes. What do you think of Belfast?
A: Well, I've only just arrived today and it's my first visit, but it seems very nice. Lots of character.
B: Are you here on business?
A: Yes, that's right. I have a meeting tomorrow. I'm a bit nervous about it.

B: I'm sure it'll go all right. How long are you staying?

A: Just a couple of days. I go back on Thursday morning. I was just looking at your paper to see how Bayern Munich did yesterday. Do you like football?

B: If it's a good match, but I'm not that keen. Actually, I prefer golf myself.

A: Do you mean you play golf?

B: That's right.

A: I play myself, but not very seriously. I find it relaxing though.

B: Yes so do I, I love spending ...

B: ... Oh, well, Allan, it's getting late. I have to be off. Thanks for the drink, and good luck with your meeting.

A: Right, it was nice talking to you.

B: It was nice talking to you too. Cheerio, then.

A: Bye.

9 The ability to end a conversation is just as important as the ability to start one. There are many reasons for wanting to end a conversation, including dislike of the person you are talking to or simple boredom with the conversation. Whatever the reason, it should be done politely, and several gambits are given here which students will find useful.

Students match the sentence halves. Check answers with the class. You may like to ask students whether they think the other person will genuinely believe the excuse that is given for ending the conversation. In most cases, they probably won't, but these are polite and accepted formulae for ending conversations which will not give offence. You might like to point out, however, that saying you've got a call on your mobile and then just turning round to talk to someone more attractive behind you would not be acceptable!

ANSWERS

a 3   b 4   c 2   d 1   e 5

10 Students work with a partner to plan their conversations. Give them a few minutes to think about what they are going to say, but don't allow them to write scripts and read them out. As they do their roleplays, go around monitoring and helping. Praise any use of the useful language they have learned for starting conversations, introducing oneself, keeping the conversation going and ending it politely.

When your student starts a conversation, react with interest to the newspaper story he / she mentions and try to get him / her to come up with some possible details for the story. It might be a good idea to demonstrate first and encourage the student to ask you for further details.

C Stick to your guns

Learning objectives

This scenario looks at the issue of staff satisfaction and whether carrying out a survey to assess staff morale is a useful procedure or a complete waste of time. Students begin by reading an extract from a business blog and discuss the questions in a staff satisfaction survey. They then watch a video in which a new staff survey is discussed and there are objections to it. Students roleplay a conversation between two people involved in setting up the survey, and prepare a short presentation to introduce it.

Digital resources: Workplace Scenario C

📹 In company in action C1–C2 and worksheet; Extension worksheets; Glossary; Student's Book answer key; Student's Book listening script; Fast-track map

Warm-up

Draw attention to the definition of the phrase ***stick to your guns*** and the example sentence in the margin. Ask students for examples of situations in which it is good to stick to your guns.

1 Give students time to read the blog and discuss the questions with a partner before reporting back to the class. Find out if any of them works in companies where staff satisfaction surveys are used.

2 📹 **C1** Go through the instructions and the questions with the class before you play the recording so that they know what information to watch out for.

ANSWERS

a They discuss i, iii and v.
b No. Ralph thinks it's a waste of time because people didn't believe it was truly anonymous so they felt they couldn't answer some of the questions honestly. Vanessa doesn't seem to have any objections to the survey.
c Students' own answers

📹 **C1**

Ralph: There you go!
Vanessa: Can I help you, Ralph?
R: These are the surveys Serena wanted us to do.
V: Is this everyone's?
R: Everyone from Sales and Marketing, yes.
V: Great, I'll pass them on to Serena. What did you think of the survey, by the way?
R: I'm not really sure. I don't understand why it was only our department that had to do it.

V: It was a trial. Serena wanted to get some feedback from our department before giving it to the whole company.
R: Oh, I see. Well, in that case, you can tell her we thought it was a waste of time!
V: We?
R: As I collected the questionnaires, I spoke to everyone that did it, and everybody felt they couldn't answer some of the questions honestly.
V: Which questions?
R: You know, questions like 'Do you agree that the senior managers demonstrate strong leadership skills?' I mean, you can't really say no, can you?
V: Of course you can, that's why you don't have to add your name. It's anonymous.
R: They can still find out who we are. Maybe if we didn't have to login before we took the survey, then people would feel they could be more honest.
V: I'll tell Serena what you said, but I'm pretty sure she'll stick to her guns on this one.
R: Okay, but don't tell her *I* said that!
V: Don't worry, I'll just say it was general feedback from the team. Thanks, Ralph!

3 Give students time to read the email and answer the questions. Check answers with the class.

ANSWERS

a He wants to discuss some things about the survey before they launch the process with the whole company.
b Open-ended questions are those that don't have a fixed answer (so not multiple choice, true/false or involving scoring) so the person answering the question is free to make comments, saying or writing what they think.

4 Go through the instructions, then tell students to work with a partner, each turning to their respective pages to roleplay the conversation using the information and useful language given. Go around monitoring and assisting where necessary.

Ask your student to choose one of the roles. You take the other.

5 Ask students to individually complete the FEEDBACK: Self-assessment section on page 135 of the Student's Book and then discuss answers with their partner. Ask students if there was anything they found surprising.

6 📹 **C2** Play the video for the students to see the conversation between Serena and Joe. Ask them to comment on how it differed from their roleplays. Then ask them to repeat their roleplays, swapping roles. Remind them to use their self-assessment notes and the useful phrases provided.

C2

Joe: Serena.

Serena: Joe.

J: Thanks for coming in. As you know, I wanted to talk to you about the trial of the staff satisfaction survey.

S: Right. Do you want to discuss the points in your email?

J: Absolutely. Firstly, what was the general feedback from the Sales and Marketing team about the survey?

S: Well, not great, to be honest. Vanessa told me that they thought it was a waste of time.

J: Oh, really?

S: Yes, but it doesn't …

J: Hang on! Just a sec. Oh, dear.

S: Shall I come back?

J: No, no, no. It's fine. Okay, sorry about that. So the feedback wasn't good?

S: That's right, they were worried about some of the questions. The problem is they didn't feel they could really be honest answering questions about senior management.

J: Did you tell them that it's an anonymous survey?

S: Yes, but according to Vanessa, they didn't believe that.

J: Yeah, I thought the question of anonymity might be a problem. So what do you suggest?

S: I'm convinced that we should go ahead with the survey anyway. After the first year, when everyone has seen that the survey really is anonymous, the staff will trust it more and they'll be happy to answer the questions honestly.

J: But for the first year we do the survey how can we convince people that it really is anonymous if they have to log in?

S: Well, I'm suggesting that all surveys that are uploaded to the system don't have any names attached to them. They just have a number, and there's no way to connect a number to a name. So we couldn't match a person's name to a survey, even if we wanted to. I'll explain this to the staff, before we ask them to take the survey. I'm sure they'll understand.

J: Okay. But I had another idea. What about using a paper form? That way people wouldn't have to log in at all.

S: I think it would be more successful in the long term if we use an online survey. It will make it easier to collect data and compare the results for each year.

J: Okay, that makes sense. Did you also consider a comments section?

S: Yes, but I think that it would be a lot better for everybody if we use questions with a score from 1 to 5, rather than having open-ended questions, or adding a comments section at the end. This way, we'll be able to get accurate data that can be compared from year to year.

J: Okay, if you're sure.

S: Definitely.

J: So, what about the other things on my email?

S: Well, apart from the things we've discussed, there's cost.

J: That's right. Should we do an internal survey or hire an external consultant to do it?

S: Internal. It will be much cheaper.

J: Are you sure we can make a survey which is as good as one created by specialists?

S: I've done a lot of research and I'm convinced we can create a very detailed survey, which will provide useful results.

J: Good. And how about the results? Do you think we should publish them?

S: I've thought about that, and yes, I think we should publish the results in our e-newsletter, so that the staff can see that we're happy to reveal the results, whatever they are.

J: Okay then. It looks like you have everything planned. Let's go ahead and do the survey with the whole company, as you suggested.

S: Great! It's all prepared, so I'll send you an email with the details later today.

J: Fantastic! Thanks, Serena.

7/8 Go through the instructions with the class, then tell students to work on their presentations with a partner. Go around giving help where needed. When the presentations are ready, get the pairs to take turns giving their presentations to other pairs and answering their questions. Encourage the listening pairs to raise objections and the speaking pairs to stick to their guns.

1:1 Get your student to make the presentation to you. Raise objections and encourage the student to stick to their guns and counter your objections.

13 Air travel

Learning objectives

With increased globalization, many people now find that they have to travel abroad on business, which means long hours on planes and at airports. This unit looks at flying and gives students useful language for the formalities of checking in for a flight and advice on how to secure the best seat. A reading text examines cut-price travel and explains the wide variety of prices paid for seats on the same flight. Finally, students take part in a negotiation game, in which they gain points by successfully negotiating such things as price, quantity and delivery date of a product.

The grammatical focus is on conditionals with *will*, and the lexical focus is on air travel and negotiating.

Digital resources: Unit 13

Online Workbook; Extension worksheets; Glossary; Phrase bank; Student's Book answer key; Student's Book listening script; Fast-track map

---

In this first section, students begin with a general discussion about flying and their attitudes to it. They then listen and complete two conversations at an airport check-in desk and identify what goes wrong in each case.

Warm-up

Focus attention on the quotation at the top of the page. Find out how many students in the class enjoy flying and if there is anyone who feels guilty about its impact on the environment.

Brainstorm as many words as students can think of which are connected with flying and arrange them in a spidergram on the board, with *flying* in the middle and different sections for things such as *airport words*, *things in a plane*, *feelings about flying*, *things that can go wrong*, etc.

Ask students to discuss the question in the margin and give reasons for which they think is the best low-cost airline and which is the worst.

1 Divide the class into small groups for this discussion. You could appoint a secretary in each group who takes notes and then reports back to the class on what was said.

2 🔊 **2.09–2.10** Tell students that the first time they listen to the recording, all they have to do is find out what the problem is in each of the two conversations. Allow students to compare their answers in pairs or small groups before checking answers with the class.

ANSWERS
In Conversation 1, the passenger has lost his electronic ticket and can't check in without the reference number.
In Conversation 2, the passenger's bag is overweight, and he has to pay a charge for excess baggage before checking in.

🔊 **2.09**
Conversation 1
A: Good morning. Is this where I check in for flight RA 264?
B: Yes. Can you give me your reference number, please?
A: I'm afraid I've lost the paper I had it on, but here's my passport.
B: I'm sorry, but if you haven't got the reference number, I can't check you in. You'll have to go to the main desk over there. They'll give it to you.
A: But can't you look it up? You've got my name.
B: I'm afraid not, sir.
A: Do I have to queue up again?
B: No. Just come to the front.
A: Okay.
B: Next, please.

🔊 **2.10**
Conversation 2
A: Can I have your reference number and passport, please?
B: Here you are.
A: You've just got one suitcase to check in?
B: Yes, this one.
A: I'm afraid it's over 15 kilos. You'll have to pay excess baggage.
B: It's only just over, isn't it?
A: Actually it's 17 kilos.
B: Are you sure? How much will it cost me?
A: It'll be £30, but you have to pay over there at the main desk.
B: What, over there? There's a really long queue. Can't I pay here?
A: No, I'm sorry. But come straight to the front when you come back.
B: Okay. Thanks.

3 🔊 **2.09–2.10** Focus attention on the words in the box and make sure everyone understands them. Students should try to complete the conversations from memory first, before listening to the recording again. When they have finished, play the recording again for them to check their answers.

ANSWERS
a check in	b reference number
c passport	d main desk
e look it up	f queue up
g suitcase	h excess baggage
i thirty pounds	j long queue
k straight to the front	

Language links

Direct students to the *Language links* section on page 84 for more exercises practising vocabulary about air travel.

Battle of the armrests

In this section, an article on how to avoid getting the worst seat on the plane is used to practise conditionals with *will*. Students also learn some useful tips on getting a good seat on a plane and making the best of a bad one.

1 Put students in groups and ask them to make a list of five dos and five don'ts for business air travellers. Encourage them to think creatively and not just to copy things from this page of the Student's Book. Have a class feedback session to share ideas. Students could write out their lists neatly on posters to be displayed in the classroom.

2 Ask a student to read the introduction aloud. Then elicit suggestions from the class as to the strategies the article might describe for avoiding the worst seat on the plane.

3 Go through the example sentences in a) with the class, pointing out that the part of the sentence with *if* is the condition and the part with *will* is the consequence, i.e. what will happen as a result of the condition. This type of conditional is known as a 'First Conditional' because there are other types. Look at the conditions and the consequences in the two lists with the class. Ask three different students to each read out one of the three First Conditional sentences given in example a), so that students hear them as complete sentences, rather than just see them as matched numbers. Then allow students to work with a partner to match the rest of the conditions to the consequences. Point out that each condition clause can combine with a varying number of consequence clauses. When checking the answers, ask students to read out their complete sentences. Other students can challenge if they think a sentence is not logical.

SUGGESTED ANSWERS

a 2, 5, 6	b 1, 4, 6	c 7
d 5, 6	e 1, 3, 5, 6, 10	f 8
g 6, 10	h 9	i 3
j 4, 6		

Language links

Direct students to the *Language links* section on page 85 for more information about conditionals with *will* and more practice exercises.

4 🔘 **2.11** Students listen and circle the combinations that the speaker mentions. When you have checked the answers, have a class discussion on whether students agree with the advice (e.g. *Do you always get on and off the plane faster if you sit at the front? Do you agree that turning up 45 to 60 minutes before a flight counts as being 'early'?*).

ANSWERS

a 2 b 1 c 7 d 5 e 10 f 8 g 6 h 9 i 3 j 4

🔘 **2.11**

Book as early as possible – within three weeks of the flight. With an early booking you can choose the seat you want. However, if you book months in advance, you'll be too early for a seat assignment.

If you use a travel agent, make sure they have a record of your seating preferences – aisle or window. Tell them you want to sit close to the front. If you sit at the front, you'll get on and off the plane faster.

When you receive your ticket and boarding pass or e-ticket confirmation, check the seat assignment. Mistakes happen. If you have time, cross reference with the airline seating chart.

If you are unable to confirm a seat, be sure to get to the airport early – at least 45 to 60 minutes before the flight.

If you do have an assignment for your preferred seat, don't check in too late. Those few minutes reading magazines at the newsstand can translate into hours of discomfort in the air.

Finally, the gate check-in attendant can be your best friend. Ask politely if there is a better seat available. Saying that you are claustrophobic might not hurt, but don't feign an illness or say you're pregnant if you're not. There's no point in feeling guilty the entire flight.

If, in spite of your best efforts, you end up with the middle seat, here are some tips to cope:

If you are late boarding and have your choice of middle seats, go for the one up front near the exit.

Check out the aisle and window passengers. Do they look like they will be self-contained and give you plenty of room? Observe their body language and trust your instincts.

Capture as much personal space as you can right away. Dominate the two armrests. This will force your seatmates to give you more space. Be polite, but establish your territory. After all, they have 'personal space' on either side.

Don't work on your laptop during the flight. A cramped space becomes even more claustrophobic when you bring out the hardware. And don't try to read a newspaper. Stick to small paperbacks.

Although it is important to keep hydrated in the air, don't drink water by the gallon. If you climb over seatmates repeatedly to get to the bathroom, they'll get annoyed.

Get up once during the flight to stretch your legs, even if you don't have to use the restroom. This time away will allow your companions to move around as well and refresh the whole row.

Buying an airline ticket

In this section, students read an article about cut-price travel which explores why people pay different prices for seats on the same plane and how discount airlines make their money. They answer questions on the article and complete sentences using information from it. They then discuss their own experiences of cut-price travel.

Warm-up

Find out who has paid the least for an airline ticket. Where did they go and how much did it cost? Ask them what the budget airlines in their country are and whether people like using them. How do they think the airlines can afford to offer seats so cheaply?

1 Go through the questions with the class before they read the article. Give them plenty of time to do this, and answer any questions about vocabulary.

ANSWERS

a Because tickets are now bought online rather than through an agent, so it is your responsibility to find the best deal.
b They only make a profit on the last nine seats booked on any flight.
c They will say that special fees on things they have to provide, such as wheelchairs and terrorism insurance, push the prices up.

2 Go through the question with the class. Tell them that their answers need to form part of a First Conditional clause, and do the first one as an example with the class. As students complete the sentences, go around offering help and making sure that they are forming the conditional clauses correctly. When checking answers, accept any that are grammatically and factually correct.

SUGGESTED ANSWERS

a will be different
b will fall
c get a bad
d they won't make a
e there are nine or more
f you will have to pay excess baggage
g you are five minutes late for check-in

3 Students work with a partner to discuss the question. Have a class feedback session to compare opinions.

4 Encourage students to say the collocations aloud as they find the wrong verbs. This will give them a feel for what sounds right and what sounds wrong. Check answers with the class.

ANSWERS

a good deal: ~~buy~~
costs: ~~delete~~
a fortune: ~~do~~
the price: ~~reserve~~

5 Check the answers to this exercise by asking students to read their corrected sentences aloud, so they hear the collocations used in context and can remember them more easily. Accept any sentences that are logically correct.

SUGGESTED ANSWERS

a increase costs/increase the price
b get a good deal
c reduce costs
d make a fortune
e increase the price
f offer a good deal, reduce/lower the price
g increase the price

The negotiation game

In this section, the focus moves away from air travel to negotiation. Students follow the instructions on the relevant pages to play a game in which they negotiate the price, quantity, delivery time, etc of a product.

Language links

Direct students to the *Language links* section on page 84 for more negotiation vocabulary.

1 Students discuss the questions with a partner, then report back to the class.

2 2.12 Go through the instructions in 2 and 3 with the class, then play the recording for students to hear two people playing the game. Point out the speakers' use of conditionals with *will* (*If I order 100 units, will you give me a price of 5.5 euros?*, etc).

> 🔘 **2.12**
> A: If I order 100 units, will you give me a price of 5.5 euros?
> B: No, I'm sorry. I can't do that. On 150 units I'll give you a price of six euros.
> A: Six euros. And what about payment?
> B: Payment is within 60 days.
> A: If we pay within 30 days, will you lower the price?
> B: I'll go down to 5.5 euros if you order 200 units or more. That's my best offer.
> A: Well, what about the guarantee?

3 Working with a partner, students decide what the product is. Student A is the buyer, and Student B is the seller. They turn to their respective pages, where they will find the instructions, a chart telling them how many points they will score for each category and a *Useful language* box. Make sure everyone understands what they have to do. As students negotiate, go around offering help and encouragement. Make a note of any particularly successful negotiations which can be performed for the class. At the end, find out who scored the most points as buyer and who the most as seller.

 Take one of the roles yourself and see how many points your student can score.

Language links

ANSWERS

Vocabulary
Air travel
1 1 a 2 f 3 b 4 c 5 e 6 d 7 g 8 j
  9 k 10 h 11 i
2 a 1 b 3 c 2 d 6 e 4 f 5

Negotiating
3 a business b price c order d discount e more f 10%
  g up h payment i accept j deal k deliver l do
4 a What will you do
  b If there's nothing on Tuesday
  c I'll ask him to take me
  d I'll ask you to take me
  e I'll just take a taxi then
  f I'll take the new metro
  g if I can get a room
  h if I can finish this report

Grammar
Practice 1
a 3 b 5 c 7 d 8 e 1 f 10 g 6 h 2 i 9 j 4

Practice 2
a will tell b needs c will be d find e will improve
f will phone g pay h will adopt i will lose j will have

Practice 3
a If you confirm your booking, you'll get a good seat.
b If you pretend you're not interested in buying from them,
  they'll drop the price.
c If you apologize to the boss, you won't have problems.
d If you drink too much on the flight, you will have to keep going
  to the toilet.
e If you don't leave for the airport now, you'll miss your flight.
f If you are rude to airport ground staff, they won't let you on
  the plane.
g If you don't study something practical, you won't get a job.
h If you work too hard, you'll get ill.
i If you take the client out to lunch, you will get his business.

14 Hiring and firing

Learning objectives

In this unit, students look at issues around getting and losing a job. In the first section, they read a newspaper article about a woman who was fired for taking part in a radio competition while she was at work. This article is used to present and practise the passive. Students then read a report giving the manager's viewpoint on the same incident and practise rewriting short texts in the passive.

The next section is about applying for a job, and students read extracts from four letters of application. They examine the formality of the language used and write a paragraph introducing their own CV.

In the next section, students look at a CV and a job advert, and listen to an interview. They decide whether or not they think the company appointed the candidate.

In the final section, they talk about wider issues around employment and relationships between workers and employers.

The grammatical focus is on the passive, and the lexical focus is on procedures.

Digital resources: Unit 14

Online Workbook; Extension worksheets; Glossary; Phrase bank; Student's Book answer key; Student's Book listening script; Fast-track map

In this first section, students read the story of Nicola Williams, who was sacked for taking part in a radio phone-in programme while she was at work. They examine the vocabulary used in the article and look at the use of the passive. They then read the manager's report on the incident, which gives an entirely different viewpoint. This report uses the passive in order to sound more formal and objective, and students go on to rewrite short texts using the passive. They then discuss the issue of sacking employees.

Warm-up

Write the words **hire** and **fire** at the top of two columns on the board and ask students what they mean (to give someone a job, and to take a job away from someone). Then ask how many other words they know that mean the same thing as **hire** and **fire** or are connected with them. If they don't know any, you could put this list on the board and ask them to decide which column they should go in: *take someone on, lay off, sack, appoint, downsize, let someone go, terminate someone's employment, recruit*.

Ask them the question in the margin about whether they have ever had to fire somebody. If they are comfortable with discussing the details, encourage them to say what happened.

1 Encourage students to make predictions based on the headline alone and not to read the article yet. Establish that a *phone-in* is a radio programme in which listeners are invited to phone the radio station and give their opinions on air. Sometimes these involve competitions or quizzes in which people can win prizes.

2 Students read the article and see if their predictions in 1 were correct. You could use the questions as the basis for a class discussion about students' reactions to what they have read, or ask them to discuss them with a partner or in small groups.

ANSWERS

The article is about a woman who was sacked for taking part in a radio phone-in while she was at work.
a–c Students' own answers

---

3 Ask students to underline the verbs in the text which mean the same as *to sack* and to discuss with a partner which verb is more formal. Point out that informal words (such as *fired* or *sacked*) are usually used in newspaper headlines because they have more impact.

ANSWERS

laid off, fired
Laid off is the more formal verb.

---

4 Again, tell students to underline the sentences in the article when they find them.

ANSWERS

a She was laid off.
b She was ordered to leave the factory immediately.

---

5 Do this exercise with the whole class to make sure that everyone understands the form and use of passive and active constructions.

ANSWERS

a *They laid her off* and *They ordered her to leave the factory immediately* are active.
  She was laid off and *She was ordered to leave the factory immediately* are passive.
b They (the management of the company)
c She (Nicola Williams)
d Nicola Williams
e The passive sentences put the emphasis on Nicola and what happened to her. The important information comes at the beginning of the sentence.
f It is omitted because it is unnecessary. We are not as interested in who did the sacking (Nicola's bosses) as who was sacked (Nicola).

Language links

Direct students to the *Language links* section on page 92, for more information on the form and use of the passive, and practice exercises to help them use the passive form correctly.

6 Students read the manager's report, which shows that there are two sides to every story. Point out the use of the passive to make a text sound more objective and formal in style. Elicit that the opposite of *objective* is *subjective*. A subjective approach implies more emotional involvement with the case. An objective account of something sticks to the facts. When you have checked the answers, ask students if they have changed their minds as a result of reading the manager's report, about whether they think the sacking was justified or not.

a was warned	b were given	c were noted
d was given	e was informed	f was asked
g was informed		

7 Ask students to name the source of the first story about Nicola Williams (*a newspaper*). Elicit that a newspaper is more likely to be sympathetic to Nicola than to the management of her company for a number of reasons: newspapers and their readers like 'hard-luck' stories and stories with happy endings; newspapers like to think they champion the ordinary person against the power of big business, etc. Ask students if they think that newspapers usually publish all the facts of a case. Students discuss with a partner or in small groups how the details of the incident are different in the two accounts. Have a class feedback session to compare answers.

The newspaper account doesn't mention that Nicola had received previous warnings about using her mobile phone at work. It also doesn't report that she became hysterical and abusive when she was told that she was sacked.
The manager's report doesn't include personal information, such as the fact that Nicola is a single mother with a six-year-old daughter.

8 The instructions here tell students to improve the texts by changing one verb into the passive. When you have checked answers with the class, ask students why they think this improves the texts. (Because the most important information is brought to the beginning of the sentence, where it is more prominent and has more impact; also because these are formal texts, and the passive eliminates the use of the pronouns *they* and *it*, which makes the original texts sound more informal.)

a 35,000 people have been laid off in the last five years, unemployment is rising, and there are social problems in the region.
b The business is a great success. New staff are being hired and it is expanding fast.
c As there was a recession and the number of orders decreased, one of the factories was closed.
d To improve margins, the new model is being made in Hungary, where labour costs are lower.
e Ford™ has several plants in Europe. One of them is in Valencia, and the Escort is produced there.
f Plans have been announced for the new industrial estate. It will cover ten hectares and create space for over 15 business ventures.

9 Go through the items in the box with the class to make sure everyone understands them. Students then discuss the question in small groups. You could appoint a secretary in each group to take notes and report back to the class on what was said. Emphasize that students can include any ideas of their own.

Applying for a job

In this section, students listen to people talking about their approach to applying for a job and match the people to extracts from their application letters. These are then examined for examples of formal language, which is appropriate for such letters. Students are invited to decide what this formal language really means. They then write a paragraph introducing their own CVs.

Warm-up

Find out what the normal procedure is for applying for a job in students' own countries. They may be interested to know that, in the UK, many jobs are advertised in the press. Some of the adverts ask people to contact the advertiser to receive an official application form. Others ask for a letter of application and a CV (curriculum vitae), which lists the applicant's personal details, education, qualifications, job experience and interests. In both cases, applicants would write a covering letter, explaining why they are interested in applying for the job and noting any relevant points that they wish to highlight from their CVs or which are not covered in either the CV or the official application form. Application letters are written in formal language.

1 2.13–2.16 Focus students' attention on the photos of the four people. Ask them to speculate on what kind of people they are. What adjectives would they use to describe them? Make sure students have read the summaries before you play the recording so that they know what to listen out for. Then play the recording and ask them to match the people to the summaries. Check the answers with the class.

a speaker 4	b speaker 3
c speaker 1	d speaker 2

2.13
Speaker 1
I think that these days you have to really sell yourself. Certainly this is what employers expect in the US. You should show them how great and self-confident you are. Modesty isn't going to get you anywhere and no one is going to mind if you exaggerate a bit and dress things up to sound more impressive. Make the potential employer feel that, although this is the job you always wanted and of course you are the ideal person for it, if they don't snap you up, someone else will. So, they had better hire you before they lose the chance.

2.14
Speaker 2

It's not often that qualifications and experience totally
match up to an advertised post, so it's preferable to
emphasize other qualities, like your willingness to
learn and the fact that you work hard. In fact, you
should be careful not to give the impression you are
over-qualified for the job. I think that employers
are often more interested in things like loyalty and
ability to fit in. A high-flier who knows too much can
create a bad working atmosphere and break a team.
Personally, I want the employer to think that I am
going to be easy to work with and won't create too
many waves.

2.15
Speaker 3

No one likes a 'big head' but, on the other hand, don't be
falsely modest either. Basically, your qualifications
and experience tell their own story, so you're not
going to impress anyone by adding a lot of adjectives
like 'excellent' and 'outstanding' to your CV. Usually
this will make an experienced recruitment officer
suspicious. It doesn't hurt to acknowledge one or
two weaknesses either – areas that you would like to
improve and you want a chance to develop. Above all,
be honest, because if you exaggerate or lie, in the end
someone is going to catch you out and you'll end up
looking stupid.

2.16
Speaker 4

People's motivations interest employers. If you want to
work for a specific company, tell them why, especially
if you are changing jobs. Valid reasons would be that
you are frustrated by the limitations of your present
post, or that you can't fulfil the potential of your
background and education. Don't whine, though, and
don't blame your current employers: you've learned a
lot with them, but it's time to move on. Tell potential
employers that you have a lot to offer, and all you
need is an opportunity to show it. If someone gives
you a break, they won't be disappointed.

2 Elicit students' reactions to the people they listened
to. Which one(s) do they agree with? Ask students to
discuss with a partner which approach they used to get
their present job, and if the approach depends on the job.
If your students are not yet employed, ask them to discuss
which approach they think would be the most successful.
Again, would this depend on the type of job? Have a class
feedback session to compare opinions.

3 Establish that these are extracts from letters of
application written by the four speakers in 1. Allow
students to work with a partner to match them to the
summaries. Then check answers with the class.

4 In letters of application, people want to make
themselves sound as good as they can, without actually
lying about their abilities, qualifications and experience.
Formal language is often used to give the impression that
something is true, without actually giving false information.
This will be demonstrated in the next section. Here it is
simply used to make the letter of application sound more
formal and impressive. Students read the extracts again and
find the formal phrases that match sentences a) to h).

5 This writing exercise could be set for homework. Make
sure that students use suitably formal language for their
paragraphs.

A job interview

In this section, students look at a job advert and the CV
of a woman who applied for it. They then listen to the
interview that she had for the job. This reveals how she
used formal language in her CV to suggest that she was
better qualified and more experienced than she really was.
Students are asked to complete phrases from the interview
and decide whether or not she would have got the job.

1 Go through the advert and the CV with the class and
explain anything they don't understand. A *resumé* is
the same as a CV and is the preferred word in American
English. Ask why they think Sara applied for the job and
whether from looking at her CV they think she would
be a suitable candidate. Don't pre-empt the recording
by pointing out at this stage that Sara has no real
management or sales experience, and that *Management
Team Co-ordinator* and *SPC Professional* are vague titles
which give no idea of the amount of responsibility she
actually had in either of these jobs.

2 **2.17** Go through the interview questions with the class so that they know what to listen out for. Make sure they understand that the interviewer will not use exactly the same words. Play the recording for students to listen and tick the questions he asks.

ANSWERS

a, d, e, h

2.17

A: Right, shall we make a start? My name is Philip Rickett. I work in the human resources department and I'm responsible for recruitment.

B: Pleased to meet you.

A: Did you find us all right?

B: Yes, the map you sent me was very clear.

A: Good. Now, this is just a preliminary interview to check out some details. If you're successful, you'll go on to a more in-depth interview this afternoon. Is that all right?

B: Yes, I don't have to be back at work until tomorrow morning, so as long as I have time to drive back this evening, that's fine.

A: Do your present employers know where you are?

B: No. I asked for a day's unpaid leave for personal reasons. I didn't say why.

A: What don't you like about your current position?

B: Actually, there are a lot of things I do like about it, but no job is perfect. I think I am ready for more responsibility and when I saw your advert, I thought I should apply.

A: You know this job is a managerial position. How much managerial experience do you have? It's not very clear from your CV.

B: Well, in my present job I'm a management team co-ordinator.

A: Yes. Does that mean you're the leader of the team?

B: Not exactly. I assist the general manager in running the department.

A: Oh, I see. Are you a kind of personal assistant?

B: No, I think it's a bit more than that …

A: But are you a manager?

B: I suppose not.

A: It says in your CV that in your previous position you were an 'SPC professional'. What exactly does that mean? Is Sales Productivity Centre basically a sales department?

B: Yes, we provided backup for 20 salespeople from different sectors of the company.

A: Are you saying you were directly involved in sales?

B: No, it was more about providing support to help drive sales and increase productivity.

A: I see. So, what sort of work did the job involve?

B: I'd say it was a position that required a lot of time management skills and prioritizing of tasks. It gave me a lot of insight into the sales process.

A: Can you be a bit more specific, please?

B: Well, to be honest, some of the work was secretarial, but I am applying for your post because I'm capable of doing far more. I'd like more responsibility and to be able to use my studies and my languages.

A: Yes, your English is obviously excellent and you speak Spanish. Is your Spanish as good as your English?

B: Yes, it's not bad.

A: Could you tell me about your degree course … in Spanish?

B: I'm sorry? Oh, I beg your pardon … Well, I need a little time to think … Let's see …

---

3 Have a class discussion about whether students think the interviewer was fair or not. How far do students think job applicants should exaggerate their qualifications and experience in order to secure an interview? The interviewer here has clearly 'read between the lines' of Sara's CV. Do they think she would even have got an interview if she had been clearer and more honest about her work experience? Find out how many students think the company would have employed Sara and how many think they wouldn't. Encourage students to give reasons for their opinions.

SUGGESTED ANSWER

The interviewer questions Sara quite closely, but he is not actually unfair. It is unlikely that the company would have employed her, as they were looking for an executive with managerial and sales experience, and Sara's previous jobs were little more than secretary and personal assistant. Also, her confusion at the end of the interview when she is asked to speak Spanish suggests that she has not been totally honest about her language abilities.

4 **2.17** Play the recording again for students to complete the phrases. Then check answers with the class.

ANSWERS

a not very clear from
b Does that mean
c Are you a kind
d are you
e It says in your CV that; exactly does that mean
f Are you saying
g what sort of work did the job
h you be a bit more

Language links

Direct students to the *Language links* section on page 91 for more exercises practising vocabulary for procedures.

5 The preparation for this roleplay could be done at home if you have little time in class. Direct students to the *Phrase bank* on page 91, where they will find useful language for asking for clarification. Go around listening to the interviews and noting any which can be performed for the class.

 Prepare your own CV so that you can do this exercise with your student.

What about the workers?

In this section, the focus turns to wider issues of employment and the relationship between workers and employers. Students look at a photo and say what is happening in it and how the situation relates to employment. They then read articles about the employment situation in two different countries and work together to match words from the article to definitions. They then discuss various issues related to employment in their country.

1 Elicit various opinions on what is happening in the photo and how the situation relates to employment and staffing.

SUGGESTED ANSWERS

Demonstrators are marching through a city.
Significance: Workers sometimes go on strike or demonstrate, usually for better pay and conditions, or to show opposition to company or government policies.

2 Students work with a partner and turn to their relevant pages. The two articles are quite difficult, so allow students plenty of time to read them and to do the exercises. In the third part of the exercise, you may need to point out that only five of the definitions relate to the five words in bold in the article. The other five definitions relate to words in the article their partner is reading.

ANSWERS

Speaker A
2 was carried out, were contacted, were paid, were frequently negotiated, were usually agreed
3 a make up for   c skilled workers   h workforce
i staffing needs   j temporary staff

Speaker B
2 will be brought to a halt, has been called, are put to them, is sacked, have been defended
3 b unemployment rate   d long-term unemployed
e workers' rights   f incentives   g unemployment benefits

 If you have limited time, this exercise could be done with the student studying only one of the articles. You can then have the discussion about the student's own country.

3 Allow plenty of time for this discussion as students will need to summarize their articles for their partners. Go around giving help, then have a class feedback session to compare ideas.

ANSWERS

Vocabulary
Procedures
1 a 1 b 7 c 2 d 9 e 4 f 8 g 5 h 10 i 6 j 3
2 a job security   b written warning   c staffing needs
   d company secrets   e workers' rights   f job application
   g skilled workers   h previous position   i unemployment
   benefits   j temporary staff   k electronics industry
3 a laid off   b down   c sack   d Firing   e verbal   f interview

Grammar
Practice 1
a The contract was signed at the end of June.
b Sheila was sacked for working too slowly.
c The office was damaged in the fire.
d Some workers were injured in the accident.
e The new measures have been announced.
f No new staff will be employed this year.
g Our corporate image is being redesigned.
h Our salaries have been increased this year.

Practice 2
a The order has been cancelled.
b The new building hasn't been finished.
c He was told about the meeting.
d The plans for the new engine were stolen.
e You will be picked up at the airport.
f He wasn't asked if he wanted the job.
g Were you told about what happened at the meeting?
h A sales conference is held every year.

Practice 3
a The light bulb was invented by Thomas Edison.
b The peseta, franc and lira were replaced by the euro in 2002.
c The United Kingdom is formed by four countries (England, Scotland, Wales and Northern Ireland).
d This book was written by Simon Clarke.
e This book is owned by (*student's own name*).
f My office is heated by (*oil, gas* or *electric*).
g The film *Avatar* was directed by James Cameron.
h The PC was originally manufactured by IBM.

15 Time

In this first section, students look at some useful collocations, discuss the link between time and money, and talk about their working hours. They also read about an unusual experiment in which a company removed all the clocks from its headquarters. They examine some vocabulary from the text before moving on to study the future with *going to* and *will*.

Warm-up

Write the word *time* on the board and ask students to tell you as many expressions with *time* and sayings about time as they can think of, either in English or in their own language. You might like to start them off with a few English sayings such as *Time flies* (*like an arrow*) and *Time waits for no man*.

Focus attention on the quotation about time management, but don't spend too long on this as it is looked at again in 3. Elicit a quick response from students, then ask them what time management skills they use.

1 Students should be able to complete these words fairly easily. When checking answers, ask students to read the whole collocation aloud so that they get used to hearing the words in combination. You could also ask them to put the collocations into sentences as you check the answers, though they will be using them to complete sentences in the next exercise.

ANSWERS

spend, save, waste, have, invest
All of the above words can collocate with *time* and *money*.

2 When students have completed the sentences, they discuss with a partner or in small groups whether the sentences are true for them or not. Have a class feedback session to compare opinions.

ANSWERS

a spend b save c have d waste

Language links ▶

Direct students to the *Language links* section on page 98 for more on the vocabulary of working conditions, and practice in using common collocations.

3 Ask students to discuss the questions with a partner and then report back to the class. Point out for question b) that Stefan Töpfer's rules are in the quotation in the margin. If you have time, you might like to ask students to add to these rules. At this point, you could ask students to say whether they are *larks* (people who have most of their energy in the morning, but tend to flag as the day goes on) or *owls* (those who are not much good in the morning, but are able to stay awake, concentrate and act energetically until late at night). If you do any team activities during this unit, you could use this division to form the teams.

4 Encourage students to read the questions first and to predict what the article will be about. This will make it easier for them the first time they read it. After students have read the article and answered the questions, allow them to compare their answers with a partner before you check answers with the class. Don't forget to elicit the students' own reactions to the article. Would they like to try the experiment in their company?

ANSWERS

a They removed all the clocks from their UK headquarters.
b To investigate how time pressure can lead to stress, and to see how an environment without clocks affects productivity.
c Because it is easy to measure.
d Because it doesn't always correspond to the natural rhythms of the human body.
e Most people carried on as normal or enjoyed the experience; one person found it disorienting; one office manager was against it and found it chaotic.

5 This could be done as a race, with the first pair of students to find all the words and phrases raising their hands. They then read out their list to the class so everyone can check their answers.

ANSWERS

a carry on b lead to c measure d drop off e hang on

6 Students work individually to complete the sentences. Point out that one answer (e) needs to be changed to the third person singular. Check answers with the class.

ANSWERS

a lead to b measure c hang on d carry on e drops off

7 Students work with a partner to discuss the sentences in 6. Make sure they give reasons for their opinions.

8 Do this exercise with the whole class, making sure everyone is clear about the use of *going to* to talk about future plans and intentions.

a the future   b We intend to bring the clocks back ...

Language links

Direct students to the *Language links* section on pages 98–99 for more presentation of the structure of *going to* for future plans, decisions and intentions.

9 Students work with a partner to make sentences using *going to* about their plans for the following day. Ask some pairs to report back their sentences to the class.

The new database

In this section, students listen to a conversation about delays in getting a new database up and running. They answer questions about this problem and complete sentences with useful vocabulary for talking about deadlines and delays. They then talk about schedules in their own companies and what they do when things are delayed.

1 Give students a minute or so to match the words and phrases and the definitions. Check answers with the class.

a 2   b 3   c 1   d 4

2 **2.18** Go through the questions with students before you play the recording, so that they know what to listen out for. You may need to point out that Domingo is the IT technician and Joe is the person who calls to find out what the delay is for getting the new database online.

a A delay in putting a new database online.
b Last October
c Next October
d He seems very relaxed about it, given that the database is severely delayed.

2.18
A: Hello.
B: Hello, is that Domingo?
B: Yes, speaking.
A: Hi, this is Joe. Look, I need you to tell me something about the new database. We're worried because it's behind schedule. What's the situation?
B: Well, yes, I'm sorry about the delay but there have been some problems with the application.
A: I appreciate that, but the system was supposed to be online last October. You didn't meet the deadline and it's now February. My boss is getting a bit nervous. And so am I.
B: Okay, okay. But you modified the requirements and the old system is not compatible with the new design. That means we have a different time frame.
A: What do you mean? How long is it going to take?

B: We need to make sure that migrating the data from the old database is going to go smoothly. We don't want to lose anything important. And then there are the security issues, but I think we should be ready by October.
A: I don't understand. Are you saying that the schedule for all this is now next October?
B: Yeah. It shouldn't take longer than that.
A: You're joking.
B: No, I'm not actually. It really is much more complicated than anyone anticipated.
A: Can you guarantee that you're giving us priority on this? Will it be on time?
B: Yeah, sure, you're at the top of the list.
A: Okay. Listen, is Jorgen there? I'd like to speak to him.
B: Hang on, I'll see if he's available.

3 💿 **2.18** Students listen and complete the phrases. You may need to pause the recording at strategic points to allow the students time to write them down. Remind them that contractions count as one word.

a behind schedule   b the delay
c didn't meet the deadline d different time frame
e long is it going to take   f the schedule
g it be on time

4 Ask students to work individually to complete the sentences so that they are true for them. Then they work with a partner to compare their answers. Ask some pairs to report back their sentences to the class.

Wasting time

In this section, students read a humorous article in which the writer recommends ways of wasting time at work without getting caught. The article is used for more practice of useful collocations and office vocabulary.

Warm-up

Find out what students' favourite ways of wasting time are. Do they play games or apps on their computers? Do they doodle on notepads? Do they stare out of the window?

1 Students match the collocations. When checking the answers, encourage students to use the collocations in sentences of their own so that they hear them in context.

a 4   b 1   c 2   d 3

2 Students work individually to complete the article introduction with the collocations in 1. When checking answers, ask different students to read out sections of the text and supply the missing words. Elicit students' reactions to the text. Do they think it is funny or shocking? Do they ever waste time at work? Why and how?

a waste time   b delicate balance   c bottom line   d get caught

3 You could ask students to work in small groups, each choosing one or two of the headings and writing short texts giving their tips for time-wasting. Read them out or display them in the classroom for the others to read and enjoy.

4 Students read the author's tips on page 142. Have a class feedback session to see if any of them are the same as the students' recommendations in 3. Have they ever done any of these things?

5 Students find words in the text on page 142 to complete the sentences. When checking answers, ask students to read out the completed sentences. Then elicit their reactions to the sentences.

ANSWERS

a in a mess   b set aside   c surf   d research   e nod

Dealing with problems

In this section, students complete conversations with *going to* and *will*. They then have similar conversations about their own plans and decisions.

1 **2.19–2.21** Ask the students to try to complete the conversations before you play the recording. By doing this, they will start thinking about language rather than just listening for the answers. Play the recording for them to check their answers.

ANSWERS

a 'm going to	b 'll start
c 'm going to take	d 'll phone
e 'm going to take	f 'll take

 2.19

Conversation 1

A: Where are you going?

B: Well, I've finished everything I had to do so I'm going to leave early.

A: What about the sales predictions for next month?

B: Oh, I'd forgotten about that. I'll start on them tomorrow first thing. I've arranged to meet someone at five.

 2.20

Conversation 2

C: Have you planned Mr Logan's visit? What about lunch tomorrow?

D: I'm going to take him to The Redwing.

C: I seem to remember he's a vegetarian.

D: Is he? In that case, I'll phone to check they have a vegetarian menu.

 2.21

Conversation 3

E: Is everything confirmed for your trip to San Sebastian?

F: Yes, the plane goes to Bilbao. I'm going to take the train from there.

E: No, don't do that – it takes forever. The bus is much faster.

F: Is it? Well, I'll take the bus, then.

2 Students read the conversations again and look at how *will* and *going to* are used. You might like to get them to highlight them in the completed conversations. If they show no understanding, give them a clue by asking *when* they think each decision was made. Then ask them to underline the correct options.

ANSWERS

a *Will*   b *Going to*

Language links

Direct students to the *Language links* section on pages 98–99 for more information about the uses of *going to* and *will*, and practice activities to reinforce the difference between the two structures.

3 Students work with a partner to have similar conversations. Go through the instructions and the examples with the class and make sure everyone understands what they have to do. You might like to highlight the different ways that the speakers in 1 introduced the problems (*What about ...? I seem to remember ... No, don't ...*), so that they don't just follow the example and use *But ... .* Weaker students may need to think of ideas for their alternative plans in advance – though these are supposed to be spontaneous decisions using *will*, so don't encourage too much preparation! Encourage the pairs to take turns being the person who says what they are going to do and the person who mentions the problem. Go around monitoring and encouraging, and note any particularly successful conversations which can be performed for the class. Encourage pairs who finish early to think up their own situations and problems.

The myth of time management

In this section, students listen to a talk on time management and put a list of topics in order. They then complete sentences from the talk, and discuss the speaker's opinions on time management. Finally, they look at the way they manage their own time.

1 **2.22** Read the topics with the class and ask students to say what order they think they should be in before you play the recording. Play the recording for students to order the topics. You may need to play it a second time.

ANSWERS

1 Introduction – Does time management work?
2 Factors beyond our control
3 Dealing with interruptions
4 Prioritizing
5 Defined tasks versus problem-solving

 2.22

Good afternoon. The subject of my presentation today is 'The Myth of Time Management'. There are thousands of books and online courses on the market which are designed to help people be better managers of their time. They all suggest techniques for using our time more efficiently. They recommend making 'to do' lists, prioritizing, and not answering the phone as ways to make us more time-efficient. But do these techniques really work?

They say that time is money, but time is not like other resources which we manage, such as materials and machines. Use of time depends to a large extent on personality and attitude, but also factors outside our control. Sometimes we can change our own behaviour, but time management really depends on changing the behaviour of the people around us and the demands they make on our time. This is always difficult and often impossible. As a result, you can be a very efficient user of your time – disciplined, organized and choosing the right moment to do vital tasks, yet still feel stressed and overworked. In fact, in many cases this is simply because you are being asked to do more than is possible in the time available.

The reality is that our use of time is usually about making choices that we don't in fact have. One of the recommended techniques is to close your door at certain times, or leave your voicemail to deal with calls. That's all very well, but if interruptions and dealing with unpredictable human problems are part of your work, then those techniques don't help very much.

Another time-management technique is to analyze what you are doing and decide if it is important or not. Well, I think most people of average intelligence can normally see the difference between activity which is useful and activity which is a waste of time. Unless they dislike their job or their employer, they will do useful things in their work time.

Time management may work with jobs with very defined tasks, where procedures and processes are very clear. Machine operators, for example, don't have to worry much about managing their time because the pace of work is imposed from outside. On the other hand, if you are faced with a task which involves creativity or problem-solving, how exactly to perform the task may not be clear. It could also be that you are in a job where you lack either the necessary skills or appropriate training to carry out your duties.

We have to remember that there will always be more work than time. This is what keeps us employed. How effectively you use your time is a question of ability, training and proper planning. But above all, it is about having a positive attitude towards your work, combined with reasonable expectations about how much you can do.

2 2.22 Students read the sentences, then listen again to complete them. When checking answers, ask individual students to read out the sentences, supplying the missing words as they go.

ANSWERS

a online	b efficient	c tasks
d voicemail	e intelligence	f operators
g problem	h expectations	

3 Discuss the questions as a class. Ask students to quote specific parts of the presentation to back up their arguments. Encourage them to give their own views where possible.

ANSWERS

On the whole, the speaker's arguments suggest they are against time-management techniques, e.g. 'Time management really depends on changing the behaviour of the people around us and the demands they make on our time. This is always difficult and often impossible.'

'The reality is that our use of time is usually about making choices that we don't in fact have.'

'(Certain time-management) techniques don't help very much.'

4 Go through the instructions and chart with the class. Students work individually to complete the 'You' column. Remind them to write down percentages reflecting the amount of time they spend on average on each activity. When they have completed their own columns, make sure students ask and answer questions to obtain the information from their partners to complete the table. Remind them that the percentages should add up to 100%. They then discuss the differences and any reasons for them. Encourage students to share what they have found with other pairs.

5 Have a class feedback session to discuss students' findings in 4.

In company interviews Units 13–15
Encourage students to watch the interview and complete the worksheet.

Language links

ANSWERS

Vocabulary
Working conditions
1 a realistic deadline b eight-hour day c sales forecasts
   d bottom line e forward planning f long hours
2 a perform b observe c specialists d productive
   e intend f decided g discussion

Grammar
Practice 1
a This evening, I'm going to meet some friends for a drink.
b They're going to employ more staff to deal with the new order.
c Are you going to meet me at the airport?
d What are you going to say at the meeting?
e Next year, I'm going to study German.
f He's going to look for a new job.
g She's not going to accept our offer.
h Are we going to take the train or the bus?

Practice 2
a I'll take the team out for lunch.
b I'll switch it off.
c I'll call the IT department.
d I'll take a taxi back to the office to collect them.
e I'll take an aspirin and go home.
f I'll ask her for her business card.
g I'll call the office and apologize.

Practice 3
a 'll order   b 're going to visit
c 'll phone   d 're going to discuss
e 're going to move f 'll make
g 'm going to leave h 'll lend

Practice 4
a information b someone c easier d learn e do
f strategy g start h urgent i time

16 Getting things done

Learning objectives

This unit is about persuading other people to do things for you – and reacting to similar requests from others. It begins by introducing language for asking for favours, and looks at ways of saying 'no' tactfully and recognizing the difference between requests, persuasion and threats.

In the second section, students study two conversations, one in which a passenger secures an upgrade when he checks in for a flight and the other in which a hotel guest makes an unsuccessful complaint about his room.

Digital resources: Unit 16

Online Workbook; Extension worksheets; Glossary; Student's Book answer key; Student's Book listening script; Fast-track map

---

In this first section, students listen to and practise short conversations asking people to do something for them and asking people to allow them to do something. They then learn how to refuse a request tactfully and practise conversations in which they say 'no' without giving offence. Finally, they re-order a conversation and identify requests, persuasion and threats used to try to persuade someone to do something she doesn't want to do.

Warm-up

Brainstorm all the kinds of favours students need to ask other people for during their working lives. Organize them on the board so that there are two sections: things you ask other people to do for you (make some photocopies for you, etc), and things you ask other people to allow you to do (borrow their car, etc). Encourage students to say how they try to persuade other people to grant them favours.

Focus attention on the quotation in the margin and ask the students what assumptions they make about people they are about to call for the first time. Then ask the question about any unexpected phone calls or emails they have received recently. Find out how they reacted to being called by someone they didn't know.

1 **2.23–2.24** Students work with a partner to complete the extracts by suggesting answers that make sense in the context. Make sure they have completed all the extracts before they listen again and compare their answers. See if any pairs had other suggestions for ways to complete the gaps.

ANSWERS

Extract 1
… 've got to …
… raining. Could you …
… you don't lose it.

Extract 2
… somewhere quiet …
Could I …
… it's free by four.

We use *Could I …?* to ask people to allow us to do something. We use *Could you …?* when we are asking them to do something.

 2.23

Conversation 1

A: Oh, look outside!

B: What's up?

A: I've got to go to the Post Office to pick something up, and it's raining. Could you lend me your umbrella?

B: Of course. As long as you don't lose it.

A: Oh, right. Don't worry, I won't.

 2.24

Conversation 2

C: Gert, I have a meeting with an agent this afternoon, and they're decorating my office.

D: Lucky you.

C: The thing is that I need somewhere quiet where we won't be interrupted. Could I use your office?

D: All right, as long as it's free by four. I've got a meeting myself.

C: Don't worry, it won't take that long.

2 Students work with a partner. They could begin by practising the two extracts in 1 before they move on to making their own conversations. Go through the prompts in the table with them first to make sure that they understand everything. As they act out their conversations, go around and make a note of any particularly interesting ones which can be performed for the class. Remind fast finishers to think of two more problems and make conversations asking for help.

> **1:1** Remember to swap roles with your student so that they get practice both in making and responding to requests.

3 **2.25** Ask students how many of the requests in 2 they would agree to. How many would they refuse, and why? Go through the instructions and the questions with the class before playing the recording. Then elicit the answers to the questions. Ask students for their reactions to Richard's attitude. Would his response be acceptable in their country? What adjectives can they use to describe him? Would they respond to the request in the same way? Try to find out which of their possessions students are happy to lend to other people and which they are not. Is it always a question of value, or are there other factors at work, e.g. sentimental attachment, dislike of other people handling personal possessions, etc?

ANSWERS

a He asks him to lend him his car.
b He refuses quite aggressively.

2.25

A: Richard, I wonder if I could ask you a favour?

B: Depends what it is.

A: I've got to go over to the warehouse to do something, and I haven't got my car. Would you lend me yours?

B: No way!

A: What?

B: I never lend my car! In any case, where's your car?

A: It's in the garage. Eh, I had a little accident.

B: And you expect me to trust you with mine?

A: It's just a minor scratch. Oh, don't worry. I'll think of something else.

4 Establish that Richard's reaction in the conversation in 3 was rather abrupt and rude, and that it is possible to say 'no' but still be polite. Students work with a partner, taking a few minutes to construct a more polite conversation which uses the phrases in the box. Check the answers by having a pair of students perform their conversation for the class. Elicit what makes this conversation more polite than the one they heard in 3 (less direct language and more hesitancy, e.g. *Well, actually … It's just that …*, giving a reason for reluctance to agree to a favour, expressing interest in and sympathy for the other person's problem).

5 **2.26** Students try to put the conversation in order and compare their answers with a partner before listening to the recording to check their answers.

ANSWERS

1 d   2 h   3 b   4 k   5 c   6 i   7 g   8 n   9 f   10 m
11 a   12 l   13 e   14 j

 2.26

A: Sandra, we need someone to answer the phone from 2.00 till 4.00 while Julia is off sick. Could you do it?

B: From 2.00 to 4.00? It's not my hours.

A: I know, but you can take the time later on.

B: It's not the time. I'll have to get someone to pick the kids up from school. Isn't there anyone else?

A: No, there isn't. Look, I know it's inconvenient, but I can't think of any other solution.

B: Well, can't we just put the answering machine on for a couple of hours?

A: Not really. It creates such a bad impression. Listen, I'd do it myself, but I've got to be somewhere else.

B: I'm sure you would, but it's not my problem, is it?

A: No, it isn't, and obviously I can't force you to do it, but …

B: But?

A: … but on the other hand, if you do it, I'll see it as a personal favour.

B: I see. I don't really have much choice, do I? I hope it's just this time …

A: Yes, in principle, yes. But you never know. Your contract is up for renewal next month. Enough said?

B: Yeah, enough said.

6 Elicit the meaning of the four words and phrases (*request* = asking someone to do something for you; *suggestion* = putting forward an idea or a plan for consideration by someone; *emotional blackmail* = persuading someone to do something that they don't really want to do by making them feel guilty if they don't do it; *threat* = telling something that unless they do something for you, you will do something bad to them). Students identify the different features in the conversation in 5. Check the answers with the class and make sure they are clear about the difference between a threat (telling someone that there will be bad consequences for them if they don't do as they're told) and emotional blackmail (playing on someone's sympathies by linking the request with your personal relationship). Ask whether students think threats and emotional blackmail are ever acceptable to persuade someone to do something. Does the context (office life or personal life) affect their opinion?

ANSWERS

a We need someone to … Could you do it?

b Can't we just put the answering machine on for a couple of hours?

c If you do it, I'll see it as a personal favour.

d Your contract is up for renewal next month. Enough said?

Upgrade

In this section, students study two conversations in which people try to get their own way. In the first, an airline passenger successfully negotiates an upgrade to business class by being charming to the check-in clerk. In the second, a hotel guest tries to get a better room by complaining to the receptionist, but his manner is rude and aggressive, and he doesn't succeed.

Warm-up

Ask students to say what kind of customer they think they are. Do they try to get what they want by gentle persuasion or do they think that the best way to get what you want is to make as much noise as possible and complain if anything is not 100% right? Encourage students to share any experience they have of getting or not getting what they wanted.

1 Elicit or explain the meaning of the term *upgrade* in the context of airline travel (to be assigned a better class of seat, e.g. moving from economy to business class, by the check-in clerk). Students talk with a partner about their own experiences of getting an upgrade. If they have had an upgrade, did they ask for it or was it just given to them? What do they think is the best way to get one, e.g. should you dress smartly, try to chat up the check-in clerk, etc?

2 **2.27** Make sure students have read the questions before you play the recording so that they know what to listen out for. Play the recording and allow students to read the script as they listen. Then elicit answers from the class.

ANSWERS

a Probably not.

b Yes, he is polite. Yes, he does get what he wants.

3 Ask students to underline phrases which the passenger uses to soften his language and sound polite.

ANSWER
I was wondering if there's any chance …; I quite understand, but I'd really appreciate it if you could …; I'm sorry to put you to any trouble; thank you ever so much

 2.27
Conversation 1
A: Good afternoon, sir.
B: Hello. I'm on flight IB 603. I was wondering if there's any chance of an upgrade to business class?
A: Well, I don't know. It depends how crowded the flight is.
B: Yes, I quite understand, but I'd really appreciate it if you could have a look. I don't mind paying the extra. It's just that I've had a really hard day, and it'd be really nice to have a bit more space and comfort.
A: Just a minute, sir.
B: I'm sorry to put you to any trouble.
A: No, that's okay. Oh, yes, there's lots of space in business class. I think we can do it.
B: Oh, fantastic. How much is that?
A: That's all right, sir. Don't worry.
B: Oh, thank you ever so much.
A: You're welcome. Have a good flight.

4 **2.28** Again, make sure students have read the questions before you play the recording. When students have listened, check answers with the class. Then elicit the differences between the two conversations (the man in the second is rather rude and aggressive, and he is not successful in getting what he wants). Ask students if they think the outcomes in the two conversations are representative of real life. Do quiet, polite and charming people usually get what they want? Is rudeness and aggression always unsuccessful?

ANSWERS
a Students' own answers
b No, he isn't polite, and he doesn't get what he wants.

2.28
Conversation 2
A: Good evening, sir.
B: Look, I'm not at all happy with the room you've given me. It's on the wrong side of the hotel. It faces onto the road and it's far too noisy.
A: I'm sorry, sir. No one has ever said anything before.
B: I can't believe that. Are you going to change it?
A: I don't think I can, sir. We're a bit full tonight.
B: Look, I'm really tired, and the last thing I want to do is argue about my room. If you don't change it, I'll tell my company not to use this hotel again.
A: I'm sorry. There's no other room available.
B: Oh, come on.
A: There's nothing I can do.
B: What about some sort of discount, then?
A: I'm afraid I'm not authorized to offer a discount on your room.
B: So, I have to pay the full price for a noisy room. Great!
A: Sir, if you want, I can call you a taxi …

5 Working with a partner, students turn to page 155 and act out Conversation 2, this time making the guest polite by using the underlined phrases from 1. If they want to introduce more variety, the students playing the guest could change the reason why the room is unsuitable. Emphasize that the students playing the receptionist should listen carefully to the guest and decide what to do, based on their impression of the guest and their feelings towards him or her. As they act out their conversations, go around and make a note of any particularly successful ones which can be performed for the class. Ask students how they feel when they are confronted by rude and aggressive people. Do they feel more inclined to give them what they want (to get them out of the way as quickly as possible) or do they resist them because they are irritated by their attitude?

 In this roleplay, the student will get the most useful practice if you let them take the role of the guest.

Change for the better

Learning objectives

This scenario is based on health and safety in the workplace and understanding strategies for bringing about change. Students begin by discussing health and safety and identifying a number of signs that can be found in a business environment. They then watch a video of a CEO explaining some changes that need to be made to the company's health and safety regulations, and identify the problems that some employees will have with these changes. They then read an email which gives advice on leading change and discuss this advice before doing a roleplay in which someone tries to persuade someone else that what is proposed is a change for the better.

Digital resources: Workplace Scenario D

In company in action D1–D2 and worksheet; Extension worksheets; Glossary; Student's Book answer key; Student's Book listening script; Fast-track map

Warm-up

Focus attention on the definition of a *change for the better* and ask students to say if they have experienced any changes in the working practices of their companies that could be seen as a change for the better. Have they experienced any which were a 'change for the worse'?

1 Give students plenty of time look at the signs and the instructions in the box. Answer any questions they may have about new vocabulary. Students match the instructions to the signs. Check answers with the class, then ask students if they can think of any examples of companies or situations where they might see these signs.

ANSWERS

Top row from left: Eye protection must be worn; Head protection must be worn; Danger construction work; Foot protection must be worn; Caution overhead load
Bottom row from left: Safety harness must be worn; Danger electric shock risk; Respiratory equipment must be worn; Hand protection must be worn

2 Students work with a partner to discuss the questions, then report back to the class with their ideas.

ANSWERS

a The blue signs tell you what you must do to protect yourself from potential hazards. The yellow signs warn you of potential dangers in the area.
b Students' own answers
c Students' own answers

3 **D1** Read the instructions and the questions with the class, making sure everyone understands the situation and the options before you play the video. After you have played it once, tell students to discuss their answers with a partner. Play it again if necessary. When you have checked answers, elicit the students' responses to the video.

ANSWERS

a ii   b   ii and iii

D1

Claudia: Good morning.
David: Good morning to you, Claudia!
C: You're in a good mood today.
D: That's right.
C: Why's that then?
D: Well, my holiday starts tomorrow. The kids are staying with my parents, so Hilda and I will have the whole week to ourselves.
C: That sounds wonderful!
D: And what's more, today's my birthday!
C: Oh, happy birthday David! I didn't know.
D: That's all right. I'm just hoping to have a nice relaxing day, and then I can …
Joe: David … morning.
D: Morning, Joe.
J: Morning, Claudia. How are you?
C: I'm fine, thank you, Joe.
J: Good, good. David, I'm glad I caught you. Can we have a little chat? There's something I need to tell you about. I'd like you to get it sorted today before you go off on holiday.
D: Today?
J: Well yes, it's very important actually.
D: I see.
J: The thing is, we heard last night that there will be a health and safety audit sometime soon.
D: I see.
J: As you know, the woodworking industry experienced an increase in the number of accidents and health problems linked to work last year.
D: Yes, I read about that.
J: Well the result is that furniture manufacturers like us will have to be even stricter when it comes to health and safety.
D: Right.
J: So, there are some changes which I need you to tell Felix and the staff about.
D: Changes, Joe?
J: Changes, David. Changes for the better, I'm sure you'll agree.
D: Okay, what are they?
J: Well, first of all, everyone who works in the factory must wear a full mask at all times.

D: Even if they're not using a machine?

J: That's right, there's too much risk from dust.

D: Felix won't be happy. He says the staff don't like wearing masks at all.

J: Well, they have to, I'm afraid ... at *all* times.

D: Full mask, all times – got it. What else?

J: The only other big change is that from now on there will be no more overtime.

D: No overtime? But that's how the factory workers make extra money.

J: We cannot have people who are tired using the machines. It's too dangerous. No overtime. That's final.

D: Felix and his team will not be happy.

J: I hear you David, but that's the way it is. Now I want you to tell Felix today.

D: I think it's going to be really difficult to ...

J: Oh, you'll be fine. It's all just leading change. No problem for you, am I right? Am I right?

D: Okay.

J: Good stuff. Oh, and David ... happy birthday, by the way.

D: Thank you very much.

4 Students work with a partner to discuss the questions, then report back to the class on their ideas. Ask students about policies on health and safety and overtime in their own companies. Do they or other people work overtime? How would they react if they were told they wouldn't be allowed to do overtime any more?

ANSWERS

a Students' own answers

b It is likely they will not be happy because their wages will be lower if they are not allowed to do overtime. They may have trouble meeting production targets without overtime, and they have already told Felix that they don't like wearing masks at work.

5 Allow plenty of time for students to read the email and consider the questions. Allow them to discuss the questions with a partner, then have a class feedback session about the possible answers.

ANSWERS

a It means advantages and disadvantages, or good points and bad points.
Pros: they will be less likely to get sick from breathing in dust and less likely to have accidents through operating machinery because, presumably, they won't be tired.
Cons: the bother of having to wear a mask all the time, which will make them hot and could mean they find it difficult to talk to each other; the fact that they will not be able to earn as much money as they did before.

b Students' own answers (Though David's job in telling the team is still a hard one, Serena's advice is probably sensible and helpful. However, point 2 is not very helpful because presumably Felix and his team have not been consulted previously about this.)

c Students' own answers

6 Students work with a partner to brainstorm their ideas. Have a class feedback session. You could put all the ideas on the board and then have a class vote on which ones are most likely to be successful.

 Be prepared to help your student by feeding in a few ideas of your own to get them started. For example, David could present the need for Felix to tell his team as a management task, so that Felix feels he is being treated as a responsible manager, rather than just having an unpleasant task 'dumped' on him.

7 Go through the instructions with the class, then tell students to work with a partner and turn to their respective pages. Students follow the instructions and use some of the useful language provided. As they perform their roleplays, go around giving help and encouragement. Make a note of any particularly good roleplays which can be performed for the class.

 Let your student play David; you play Felix. Raise some objections to the news you are given, but don't be too aggressive. Remember that your English is much better than your student's and you need to help them to experience success!

8 Ask students to individually complete the FEEDBACK: Self-assessment section on page 144 and then discuss their responses. Ask if students found anything surprising.

9 📹 **D2** Play the video, then tell students to discuss with their partners how the video differed from their own roleplays. Then ask them to swap roles and repeat the roleplay. Remind them to use as many of the useful phrases as they can.

 Let your student play David again, rather than swapping roles. This will give them the chance to improve on their performance from last time.

📹 **D2**

Felix: Knock, knock. Do you mind if I come in?

David: Felix! Hi, come in, come in.

F: Is everything all right, David? You look worried.

D: No, no, I'm fine. Everything's fine.

F: That's good. It's not much, but the team and I wanted to say ... happy birthday David!

D: Gosh! Wow ... that's so kind. And look, you've all signed it. To our favourite boss ... Thank you, Felix.

F: It's nothing. Don't mention it. So, what did you want to see me about?

D: The thing is, we're going to have a health and safety audit soon.

F: When?

D: We're not sure at the moment. We only heard last night. As you know, health and safety is very important for the woodwork industry in general. The machines can be dangerous and the dust can cause all sorts of health problems.

F: Is this about masks again?

D: Yes and something else. Because of the audit and because there was an increase in accidents and health problems in this industry last year, we've decided to make two big changes that will affect the factory workers.

F: Changes?

D: That's right, and in the long term they *will* be changes for the better. And let me just say that with your help, Felix, I'm sure we'll be able to put these changes into place without too many problems.

F: Okay.

D: The first change, as you've guessed, is that from now on all workers will have to wear full masks at all times when they're working in the factory.

F: Oh, come on! We already wear half masks at the machines. That's enough, surely!

D: I'm afraid not. There's too much risk from the dust. I need you to make sure that all of the staff do this at all times.

F: It's ridiculous!

D: I know it will be difficult for you to tell the staff, and I want you to know that I will support you if there are any problems. But, let me tell you the second change. This will be bad news I'm afraid.

F: Go on.

D: In future, there will be no more overtime.

F: What? No ... what? No overtime? How will we get the work done if there's a rush?

D: It's going to mean a lot more careful planning, and there will be difficulties, but as a health and safety measure we can't have tired workers operating those machines. It's too dangerous.

F: I don't think you've thought this through, David. The factory workers need overtime to make extra money. It's very important to them.

D: I know. I realize that this will be very unpopular with the team, and I'm going to need your help in communicating these changes. When it comes to leading change like this, Felix, the senior management are very grateful for support people like you can gain from the workforce. If you help us to make the staff understand why we have to make these changes, I'll be happy to give you more managerial tasks in the future.

F: Well, I am looking for more responsibility.

D: I know that, and this could be very good for you. So, when you talk to the team I think you should make sure that you point out the pros as well as the cons.

F: What pros?

D: Well, if we make these changes, we'll do very well with the health and safety audit, which is good for the company in the long term and could affect bonus payments. But most importantly, health and safety rules are there for a very good reason; we don't want there to be any accidents or health problems in our factory, do we?

F: No, of course not. But David, I think people will be very worried about the money situation in particular.

D: Yes, I know. I'd like you to give me some feedback from the team as soon as you've spoken to them. I've postponed my holiday so I'll be here next week to help you deal with any problems. Do you think you can help me with this, Felix?

F: Yes, of course. I'll talk to them, but I don't think it will be easy.

D: I'm sure you'll do a good job and, like I said, I'm here if you need anything.

10 Go through the instructions and the list to make sure students understand what they have to do, and all the possible situations. Students work with a different partner to prepare their roleplays. When they have finished, tell them to swap roles and repeat the roleplay. Remind fast finishers that they should devise some scenarios of their own and roleplay them.

1:1 Take turns with your student to play the different roles so that now they can have practice in responding to change.

17 Office gossip

Learning objectives

This unit uses the topic of office gossip and small talk at work to practise reported speech. Students also look at the wider implications of office gossip and discuss whether it is harmful or productive. A text about an attempt to ban gossiping at work leads to a roleplay in which a management consultant tries to persuade a client to abandon a strict policy aimed at discouraging gossip at the coffee machine.

The grammatical focus is on reported speech and the lexical focus is on relationships at work.

Digital resources: Unit 17

Online Workbook; Extension worksheets; Glossary; Phrase bank; Student's Book answer key; Student's Book listening script; Fast-track map

In this first section, students listen to and discuss some office gossip. They then examine the language used and explore how we report speech and how we use *say* and *tell*. They do further work on question words and tenses in reported speech and then complete conversations and report them.

Warm-up

Focus attention on the quotation at the top of the page. Ask whether the writer thinks gossip (informal chit-chat, often about other people) is a good thing or a bad thing (good; she thinks companies should encourage it by providing communal areas where employees can talk). Then brainstorm the sorts of things people gossip about at the office and make a list on the board. Encourage students to say when and where they think most gossip in the office is exchanged (at the coffee machine, in the canteen, in the toilets, etc) and whether they think it is important for employees to have communal areas where they can share information and build up personal relationships.

1 🔘 **2.29** Make sure students have read the questions before you play the recording so that they know what information to listen out for. Ask students to speculate on what the conversation will be about. Then play the recording and check answers. Play the recording a second time if necessary. You could make the final question a class discussion.

ANSWERS

a She has been away on holiday.
b The company is planning to restructure.
c Their boss
d They have heard that some people will lose their jobs in the restructuring.
e They think she may be having an affair with Gary and that because of her 'special relationship' with him, her job will be safe.
f Students' own answers

🔘 **2.29**

A: Hi Quin. How's it going?
B: Trixy! Where have you been?
A: I had a few days' holiday owing to me.
B: Go anywhere interesting?
A: I wish! No, I went up north to stay with my parents.
B: So, you haven't heard the news.
A: What news?
B: About the 'restructuring'.
A: What restructuring?
B: They want to reorganize marketing and sales.
A: No! Really? Is it official?
B: No, but somebody overheard Gary talking to one of the management consultants.
A: What did he say?
B: Apparently he said that we were overstaffed in some areas.
A: Never!
B: Yes, this consultant told him they would have to let some people go.
A: But that's awful.
B: Yes, Gary asked him how many people it involved.
A: And what did he say?
B: He said it depended on individual performance and attitude.
A: Does that include Maureen?
B: What do you mean?
A: Well, you know what they say about her and Gary.
B: Go on …
A: I'm not saying who, but someone told me he often sees them in the Café Au Lait.
B: That little café on Oxford Road?
A: That's right.
B: Well I never! The other day he asked her if she would stay behind to work on a report.
A: There you are, then. There's no smoke without fire.
B: Listen, don't tell anyone I told you.
A: Now, come on, Quin, you know me better than that.
B: Back to work, then.
A: Right. Catch you later.
B: Bye.

2 🔘 **2.29** Go through the example sentence with the class. Elicit what has happened in the change from direct speech to reported speech (the tense of the verb has shifted back from Present Simple to Past Simple, and the pronoun has changed from *you* to *we*). Establish that the first sentence in each pair (a–e) is what the person actually said, and the second sentence is the reported speech. With stronger students, ask them to try to complete the reported speech before they listen to the recording again. Students listen again and complete the reported speech sentences. When you have checked answers, ask students to identify and underline the parts of the sentences which changed when they were reported. You may need to point out that in sentence d), the verb *sees* has not shifted back a tense. This is because it is describing something that is still happening on a regular basis: he often sees them together in the café. The speaker wants to emphasize the continuing nature of this fact and so chooses the Present Simple rather than the Past Simple.

ANSWERS

a told him they would
b asked him how many people
c said it depended
d told me he often sees
e asked her if she would

Language links

Direct students to the *Language links* section on pages 109–110, for more information on direct and reported speech and how words change from one form to the other. There is also a further transformation exercise to practise reporting what people have said.

3 Ask students to work with a partner to decide which sentence needs *said* and which needs *told*. Check answers with the class and elicit the difference between the two verbs (*say* doesn't take an indirect object; *tell* does – *he told me, we told them*, etc). Ask students to produce one or two example sentences of their own using *say* and *tell*.

ANSWERS

a said   b told
Say doesn't take an indirect object, but *tell* does.

Language links

There is a further exercise to practise the use of *say* and *tell* in the *Language links* section on page 110.

4 Complete the three sentences on the board with the class. Elicit that we only use *if* when we report *yes/no* questions. Ask students for one or two more examples of their own. You could divide the class into two teams and have them take turns to say a question for the other team to report. Each team gets a point for every correctly reported question. To make this more challenging, ensure that the questions are a mixture of questions with question words and *yes/no* questions. You may want to point out to students that it is also possible to use *whether* instead of *if*, but only do this if they can use *if* correctly.

ANSWERS

a where   b when   c if (/ whether)
We use *if* in *yes/no* questions.

5 Remind students of the tense shift they saw in 2 and ask them to complete the two sentences. Then check the answers with the class and elicit answers to the questions below the sentences.

ANSWERS

a was   b would start
The Present Simple becomes the Past Simple.
Will becomes *would*.

6 **2.30–2.33** Emphasize that students can complete the four conversations with any words that make sense in the context. Allow them to compare their answers with a partner. Then play the recording for them to listen and compare their version with the recording.

ANSWERS

a have you finished	b sorry
c excuse	d speak to
e straight away	f a minute
g discuss	h computer
i key	j ready
k okay	l look at
m busy	n you know
o quiet	p work
q suppose	r See you
s How are	t pleased
u head	v Sixty grand
w company car	x drinks

 2.30

Conversation 1

A: Jeff, have you finished last month's production figures?

B: No, Jane, I'm sorry. Can I give them to you this afternoon?

A: It's no good being sorry. There's always some excuse. If they're not on my desk by four o'clock, I'll have to speak to Mr Bradley.

B: Yes, Jane. I'll start straight away.

2.31

Conversation 2

C: David, have you got a minute? There's something I want to discuss with you … in my office.

D: What's it about?

C: Oh, well, we're missing a laptop computer from the store.

D: What has that got to do with me?

C: Well, you are the only other person with a key to the store and …

2.32

Conversation 3

E: Marie, the figures you need are ready.

F: Thanks, Pedro. Is everything okay?

E: Yes, no problems. Would you like to look at them with me?

F: Yes, but I'm a bit busy this afternoon.

E: Me too. Er, do you know that new café they've just opened? It's nice and quiet. We can go through them there after work.

F: Oh, I suppose so, but I won't be able to stay for long.

E: Great. See you there at about six, then?

F: Yes, all right. See you there.

2.33

Conversation 4

G: Hi, Monica.

H: Oh, hello, Jim. How are things going?

G: Great. In fact, you can be the first to congratulate me.

H: Yes, you look very pleased with yourself. What's up?

G: I'm the new head of the eastern sales team.

H: Oh, really? What salary are you on now, then?

G: Sixty grand a year.

H: I can't believe it. Sixty thousand!

G: And they're giving me a new company car.

H: Oh really? Congratulations, then. The drinks are on you. See you later.

G: Yes. Bye.

7 Students work with a partner and take turns to report the conversations they heard in 6. As students practise their conversations, go around offering help and encouragement, and make a note of any particularly good conversations which can be performed for the class.

> **Language links**

Direct students to the *Language links* section on page 109, for more vocabulary on relationships at work. There is also a crossword puzzle on the same topic.

Time to talk

In this section, students begin by reading a newspaper article about a new law against gossiping introduced by a Brazilian city council. They discuss the law and look at some of the vocabulary used in the article. They then discuss the subject of gossip, and talk about policies in their own companies. Next, they read a selection of website comments on the subject of gossip, and complete sentences to give their own point of view. Then they listen to a radio interview about gossip and discuss statements about it. Finally, they do a roleplay in which a management consultant tries to persuade a client to relax a strict policy banning gossip at work.

1 Give students a few minutes to read the article and discuss it with a partner. Students answer the questions. Have a class vote on whether the ban on gossiping is a good idea or a bad one. Would students like to introduce a ban on gossiping in their English classes?

ANSWERS

a The new law says that anyone who spreads gossip or rumours about work colleagues can be sacked.

b Students' own answers

2 Students scan the article quickly to find and underline the matching words and phrases. Check answers with the class, then ask students to use the new words in sentences of their own.

ANSWERS

a banned from

b spread rumours/gossip

c face the sack

3 Put students in small groups. Appoint a secretary in each one to take notes of the discussion and report back to the class.

ANSWERS

Students' own answers

4 Go through the table headings with the class before they read the comments. Then ask them to read the comments and classify them according to the headings (make sure they understand that *mixed feelings* means you aren't sure whether gossip is always good or always bad). Allow students to compare their notes with a partner before you check answers with the class. Elicit which, if any, of the comments they agree with.

SUGGESTED ANSWERS

Gossip is good: A, D, H

Mixed feelings: B, E, G

Gossip is bad: C, F

5 Ensure that students understand that they should complete the sentences with their own ideas, not the words that were used in the text in 4. Ask them to compare their completed sentences with a partner or small groups. Have a class feedback session to compare opinions.

ANSWERS

Students' own answers

6 Students work individually to match the words and the definitions, then compare their answers with a partner. When checking answers with the class, you could ask students to use each expression in a sentence.

ANSWERS

a 3 b 5 c 6 d 4 e 1 f 2

7 Read the statements with the class. You could ask students to raise their hands if they agree with each statement. Alternatively, have everyone stand up, read out the statements one by one, and ask students who agree with each one to remain standing and those who disagree to sit down. Make a note of the majority view on each one.

8 2.34 Play the recording. Ask students to make a note about whether the speaker agrees with their own opinions in 7 or not. Have a class feedback session to compare results.

2.34

A: In this week's *Business Today*, we talk to Karina Schmidt. Karina is the author of a report by the Industrial Society which looks at workplace relations, and how they've changed over the years. Karina, first of all, welcome to the programme.

B: Thank you, it's a pleasure to be here.

A: In your report, you say that many companies nowadays have abandoned some useful institutions which allowed for social interaction.

B: Yes, these days there's less opportunity to gossip and socialize. For example, often the tea trolley has been scrapped, and having a chat in the tea break was an important part of the working day. Going for a drink after work is another example.

A: And why do you think these things have disappeared?

B: I think it's all part of the revolution in human resources. Some of these traditions have become unfashionable. Talking about things not connected to work is now seen as bad and as wasting time. There are even theories about removing chairs from meeting rooms, so that the meetings are more efficient and finish quickly.

A: And are we more efficient now, then?

B: Well, that's a good question, but in any case, something has been lost from the workplace which is very important. And perhaps in the long term, with these drives for efficiency, companies are making false economies.

A: In what way?

B: The difference between a good job and a bad job are the human, emotional elements. In other words, happy employees are productive employees. People enjoy the social aspects of work, the personal interaction with colleagues, the friendships ...

A: And the gossip!

B: And the gossip. Yes, in some ways gossip is the glue that holds the organization together. Providing communal space such as coffee areas or lunch rooms allows employees to share information and build relationships that benefit both the company and the employees.

A: Are you saying that gossip should be encouraged?

B: Not exactly, it's obviously a question of balance. All gossip and chatting doesn't make for an efficient company, but neither does no gossip or chat. All I'm saying is that I think companies would do well to remember this when trying to improve efficiency and bring down costs.

A: Karina, I'm afraid that's all we've got time for. Thank you very much for talking to us. It's been very interesting.

B: Thank you for inviting me.

A: That's all for now from *Business Today*. So, until next week, goodbye.

9 Students work with a partner to do the roleplay. Give them plenty of time to prepare what they are going to say, but discourage them from writing out a script. When they do their roleplays, go around offering help and encouragement. At the end, find out how many of the managers were convinced by the consultant's arguments and persuaded to change their policy.

10 The memo is easiest to complete if, in the roleplay in 9, the personnel manager believed the policy should be changed. However, you could give students the option of backing the policy in spite of the evidence from the Industrial Society's report.

Language links

ANSWERS

Vocabulary

Relationships at work

1 a coffee machine   b management consultant
  c meeting room   d company policy   e human resources

2 1 workplace   2 drive   3 gossip   4 effort
  5 spread   6 news   7 smoke   8 office
  9 approve   10 drink   11 share   12 trolley

Grammar

Practice 1

a were
b had spent
c would
d was
e had worked
f could
g were
h would

Practice 2

a She says she's really enjoying her job at the moment.
b I said (that) it was too late to cancel the meeting.
c He told me (that) they were having a lot of problems with the production department that day.
d He asked what time Mr Keegan was going to arrive.
e He keeps telling me (that) we should buy a new computer system.
f She asked if/whether Mr Merchant was available.
g She said (that) the fixed costs included the office rent and equipment hire.
h They asked me where I worked now.
i She said (that) she would meet me at the airport at eight o'clock.
j He told me (that) he wanted to see me about the arrangements for the following day.
k He asked me if/whether the office opened on Saturdays.
l She asked when the documents would be ready.
m He keeps saying (that) he's the best salesman in the company.
n He asked if/whether he could make a phone call.
o He asked me what I thought of the new website.

Practice 3

a tell   b say   c say   d says   e told   f ask
g say   h ask   i tell; say

18 E-commerce

In this first section, the topic of e-commerce is introduced by looking at people's reasons for buying things and the factors which affect their decisions. Students discuss their own attitudes to shopping and listen to an extract from a radio programme in which experts discuss e-commerce. Students complete notes and look at ways of expressing different points of view.

Warm-up

Focus attention on the quotation at the top of the page and ask students how much shopping they do online. Encourage them to talk briefly about their experiences of online shopping, but don't go into too much detail as they will have further opportunities to share their experiences in 2.

1 Allow students to work with a partner or in small groups to discuss and complete the sentences. Make sure they have made firm decisions before they check their answers with the sentences on page 136. Have a class feedback session to find out if they agree or not.

2 Students discuss the questions with a partner, then report back to the class on what they said. Ask anyone who has bought something on the Internet to tell the class about it. Did they have any problems in doing so? Were they happy with the item when it arrived? Did the experience encourage them to buy again from the Internet, or did it put them off? What are the advantages and disadvantages of buying things in this way?

3 Go through the list of features with the class. Make sure that everyone understands them before students work with a partner and make their decisions. Remind students that some features can be positive for both the customer and the seller. Encourage them to add their own ideas at the bottom of the table. Have a class feedback session to compare results.

SUGGESTED ANSWERS

	+	−
open for business 24×7×365	S C	
competitive pricing	C	S
no need for physical premises	S	
low selling costs	S	
updated stock information in real time	S	
credit card payment	C	S
fast communication with client	S C	
cost and time of delivery	C	
collection of marketing data	S	
uncertainty about delivery		C
difficulty of returning goods		C
not good for perishable goods		S
online information limited to text and photos		C

4 **2.35** Play the recording and ask students to tick any of the ideas in 3 that are mentioned. Find out if the experts agree with students' assessment in 3 of the advantages and disadvantages of e-commerce.

ANSWERS

Open for business 24×7×365: advantage for customers.
Competitive pricing: advantage for customers and sellers.
Credit card payment: disadvantage for customers (security worries) and sellers (cost).
Cost and time of delivery: advantage for customers (convenience) and disadvantage (cost, have to wait in for delivery).
Difficulty of returning goods: disadvantage for customers.
Not good for perishable goods: disadvantage for customers.
Online information limited: disadvantage for customers.

2.35

I: For most listeners, Amazon, eBay™ and PayPal will of course be household names, and bring to mind books, music and shopping on the world wide web. According to latest surveys, three out of five Europeans have at some time bought goods on the Internet and online sales have doubled annually over the last five years. But will this growth continue? And what will the state of online trading and shopping be ten years from now? Our guests today – Paul Bradley and Johan Webb – are both well-known commentators and bloggers on business and online technology. Paul, how do you see the future of e-commerce? What are the pros and cons?

P: It's difficult to say because things move so fast, but I think the future is quite bright. I'm pretty sure that e-commerce will become the normal way to buy and trade, not in all products, but in a fairly wide range of goods. The advantages for the customer are obvious: access to products that may not be available locally, in online shops open 24 hours a day, seven days a week and 365 days a year, with delivery to your doorstep.

J: Yes, for the customer the benefits are clear – convenience and lower prices. And the seller can do business with anyone in the world connected to the Internet. In fact, the only limitations are transport and delivery costs.

P: That's absolutely right, but there are other drawbacks as well. When you buy online you have to wait for the goods to arrive – a lot of us just don't have the patience. There is also the possibility the goods won't arrive as expected and when there are problems they can be difficult to sort out. Returning goods is not easy. With a product like a computer or high-definition TV for example, people like to have a shop where they can take it back to if something goes wrong. After-sales service is still a negative factor.

J: On the plus side, the seller can deal directly with the manufacturer and offer a cheaper price as a result. For the customer, of course, the price difference has to be enough to make it worth taking the risk.

I: Is payment a problem?

P: For me, security is still the big issue in people's minds. They're scared of identity theft and what happens to the information they give online. For the moment it's something which is slowing down growth.

J: There are solutions out there. Payment systems like PayPal offer guarantees and security. If something goes wrong you can get your money back quite easily.

I: What about the type of products that can be sold?

J: Well, except for perhaps making your order at the local supermarket via a webpage, I don't think buying food is ever going to take off. Books and DVDs are one thing, but fruit and vegetables are another.

P: Yes, and buying online makes the groceries more expensive, so what's the point? Actually, this highlights another limitation. You can see pictures, read text and hear sounds on the Internet, but you can't smell a flower or feel the quality of cloth online. There will always be some products that people will want to touch and feel before they buy.

J: Not only that, but when you go to a shop and pick something up, you choose what to look at and how to look at it. On the Internet, you only see what the seller wants you to see. That's why people are more comfortable buying products like DVDs, books and electronic gadgets. Often you've already seen them in a shop before and you're just looking for a better price. Personally, for example, I won't buy clothes online unless I know it's something I want because I've been able to try it on to see if it fits.

I: Can we go back to the use of credit cards? Apart from security, are there any other issues?

P: Well, yes. Credit cards are an added cost for the seller, but you can't pay cash over the Internet.

J: There's another point here. Because payment is by credit card, very small or very large transactions tend not to be conducted online.

P: And that brings us back to what e-commerce is all about: buying and selling products which are suitable for package delivery, where, compared to traditional retail, the costs of selling, payment and transport make it worth doing business online for both buyer and seller.

J: Well, Paul, Johan, thank you both very much. If you would like to comment on anything you've heard, don't forget you can email us at …

5 **2.35** Go through the instructions with the class and make sure they understand that there is one gap for each word. Ask them to first try to complete the phrases without listening to the recording again. Then play it for them to check their answers and complete any remaining gaps.

a of e-commerce? What are the pros and cons?
b for the customer are obvious
c the benefits are clear
d there are other drawbacks
e still a negative factor
f plus side
g still the big issue
h this highlights another limitation
i only that, but
j another point here

6 **2.36** Read the two examples aloud with the class. Explain that this structure is used for contrast and emphasis. The implication is that X may be true/a good idea/easy, but Y is quite different. Point out that where the prompts have verbs rather than nouns, a gerund is needed. Then ask students to work individually to complete the exercise. Allow them to compare answers with a partner before playing the recording for them to check their answers. Encourage them to copy the intonation of the recording, which emphasizes the comparison by stressing the words *one* and *another*.

For answers see Listening script below.

2.36
a The right qualifications for a job are one thing, but having experience is another.
b A high turnover is one thing, but making good profits is another.
c Having a good idea is one thing, but putting it into practice is another.
d High productivity is one thing, but improving staff motivation is another.
e Creating a good product is one thing, but selling it is another.

7 Students work with a partner to brainstorm the advantages and disadvantages of each pair of things. Have a feedback session to compare ideas.

8 Put students into groups of three. Students could decide which roles they are going to take, and do their preparation for the roleplay at home. If you do this in class, they will need sufficient time to prepare properly. In either case, allow them to make brief notes on what they are going to say, but don't allow them to write out scripts. In their roleplays, they should listen and respond to what the other members of the focus group say, as well as contributing their own opinions. Go around offering help and encouragement.

 To do this roleplay with only one student, omit role C and ask the student to play either A or B, with you taking the opposing role. You could then do it again, swapping roles. Whatever role you take, you could also fulfil the role of the focus group leader, asking questions and leading the discussion.

The future of the Internet

In this section, students look at some useful vocabulary for talking about the future of the Internet, then look at some statements and decide whether or not they agree with them. They compare their answers with the views of some experts, then use some of the new vocabulary to complete statements.

Warm-up
Ask students to brainstorm a list of the things you can use the Internet for. They have already looked at Internet shopping. Encourage them to come up with as many different ideas as they can.

1 Working on these words will give students a head-start when they read the survey in 2. When checking answers, encourage them to say if they have any experience of any of these things.

ANSWERS

a 3 b 1 c 6 d 5 e 8 f 2 g 4 h 7

2 Students work with a partner, reading each statement and discussing whether or not they agree with it. Tell them to mark the final column with a tick or cross, as appropriate. Go around helping with anything they don't understand.

3 Before turning to page 137, have a class feedback session on students' answers to 2. Work out what percentage of the class agrees and disagrees with each statement. Put the results on the board and then ask students to turn to page 137 and find out what the experts thought. Give them time to digest the information and then ask them if they found anything surprising.

4 Students complete the statements individually. Check answers with the class.

ANSWERS

a portable
b privacy
c tolerant
d Copyrighted content
e reliable
f augmented reality
g voice-recognition
h virtual office

5 Ask students to discuss the statements in 4 with a partner or in small groups, and decide whether or not they agree with them. Have a class feedback session to compare opinions.

6 Read the example aloud to the class, focusing attention on the use of *will* for future predictions. Ask students to underline the other predictions which use *will* (or *won't*) in the survey on page 113.

ANSWERS

The mobile phone (or smartphone) will be the primary Internet connection …
People will be more tolerant than they are today …
… will help them learn about other people.
There will be less violence and fewer wars.
There will be strict controls on copyrighted content …
People who use copyrighted materials will automatically pay …
Internet service providers will notify authorities …
People will be more open …
The concept of privacy will change …
… people will become more responsible for their own actions.
Virtual worlds and augmented reality will be popular …
Most well-equipped Internet users will spend some of their day …
It will be more difficult to distinguish …
As all phones, tablets and computers will have built-in voice-recognition …
… it will be completely normal to hear people talking in public to their computing devices.
… these devices will allow you to display …
… it will be common to see people 'air-typing' …
The Internet will still have its original architecture and won't be replaced …
It will be more reliable and secure …
Those who want to commit crimes … will still be able to do so.
The separation between work hours and personal time will disappear.
People won't depend on fixed timetables …
They will perform both their professional and personal duties …
… which will often be a virtual office.

7 Ask two students to read the example conversation aloud. Students practise it with a partner, then discuss the other predictions in the survey on page 113 in the same way. Go around offering help and encouragement.

8 In this freer exercise, students are invited to make their own predictions about the future of the Internet. Give them time to think about this, then elicit suggestions and write them on the board. Make sure that students use *will* correctly in their predictions.

Language links

Direct students to the *Language links* section on pages 115–116, for more information on *will* for future predictions.

9 Go through the example conversation with students. Explain that they can use this as a model for talking about the other items in the table. Students then work individually to decide whether or not they think the predictions will come true. They then discuss them with a partner, using the example conversation as a model. Fast finishers can make other predictions and discuss them with their partner.

Language links

ANSWERS

Vocabulary

Shopping and the Internet

1 a 4 b 5 c 2 d 1 e 6 f 3
 a compare prices b run up a bill c try on a sweater
 d access a network e listen to the conversation f influence the decision

2 a online b website c download d email
 e security f button g clicked h message
 i crashed j came k reply l pay m charge
 n complain

Grammar

Practice 1

a Prices will continue to rise.
b There will be a boom in the economy.
c The managing director will retire with a massive golden handshake soon.
d The government will take measures against inflation.
e Young George will have a very successful career, I'm sure.
f The company will go public by next year.
g Life here will get better.
h The plane will arrive late as usual.
i The political situation will affect the economy.

Practice 2

a You won't have any problems with the new system.
b I think you'll find the information on the Internet.
c I think you'll have a good time in Berlin.
d I don't think you'll see Juan Montes there.
e Do you think you'll have time to write the report?
f What time will you arrive?
g How long will it take us to get there?
h I don't think we'll have any time to go shopping.
i I think he'll make a lot of money.
j Most people will always want to see products before they buy them.

Practice 3

a What time do you think you'll get home tonight? About 7.30.
b What time do you think you'll have dinner?
c Where do you think you'll go on your next holiday?
d Do you think you'll change jobs in the next five years?
e Do you think you'll lose weight this month?
f How long do you think it'll take to do this exercise?
g Do you think you'll ever have your own business?
h Do you think you'll ever drive a Ferrari?
i Do you think you'll work as hard five years from now?

19 E-work

Learning objectives

This unit explores the issues around telecommuting (working from home), something which has been made more possible in recent years because of advances in computer technology and changing attitudes to working styles.

Students begin by looking at an article about the rise in telecommuting, which reports on a survey of people's attitudes to it.

Next, the focus turns to the experiences of people who work at home, and students look at two case studies. They listen to interviews with the people and complete a chart about their work. Then they discuss the advantages and disadvantages for them of working from home. This leads into a text on the advantages and disadvantages of home-working, and students examine some of the vocabulary used in this text.

In the next section, students discuss an advert for e-work on the Internet and look at the advantages and disadvantages of this kind of work. This leads into a study of conditional sentences for talking about hypothetical or imagined situations.

Finally, students take part in a roleplay between the manager of a company who wants to introduce a system of working at home and a union representative who is against it.

The grammatical focus is on conditionals with future reference, and the lexical focus is on teleworking.

Digital resources: Unit 19

Online Workbook; In company interviews Units 17–19 and worksheet; Extension worksheets; Glossary; Phrase bank; Student's Book answer key; Student's Book listening script; Fast-track map

Warm-up

It may be helpful to establish a definition of two key terms used in this unit. *E-work* refers to work done away from the office using a computer and a telecommunications link, either by company employees or self-employed workers. *Telecommuting* refers to any kind of work done away from the office, which may or may not involve a computer. Find out how common working from home is in students' country/countries and in their particular industry – and how popular it is with employees and employers. If any of them has experience of working from home, ask them to tell the others about it and whether they prefer it. Is it easy for them to get down to work, or do they find it distracting to be in their home environment? Do their partners or children interfere in their work in any way? Do they think they get more done at home or in the office?

1 Students work with a partner to discuss the questions, then report back to the class on their answers.

2 Ask students to read the article and compare the author's findings with their answers in 1.

ANSWERS ACCORDING TO THE ARTICLE

a Working from home
b All kinds of workers telecommute. The survey suggests that higher management positions are more suited to telework.
c Yes, it is.
d It is valued so highly that many would be prepared to give up some of the perks of their job and some would even be prepared to take a cut in salary to be able to do it.

3 Ask students to work individually to decide whether the statements are true or false, according to the article. Then allow them to compare their ideas with a partner before checking answers with the class.

ANSWERS

a T   b F   c F   d T   e F   f F   g F

4 Ask students to discuss with a partner which figures they find surprising. Then compare as a class.

Working at home

In this section, students listen to two interviews with people who telework. Their circumstances are quite different. Students match items to the speakers and then complete a chart about their jobs. They then discuss the advantages and disadvantages that working from home would have for them personally, before moving on to a text that lists some of the good and bad points of teleworking. They look at some of the vocabulary in the text and use it to complete sentences.

Warm-up

Ask students if they think there are any jobs that can be done totally from home. Are there any in which they think it would be impossible to do any part of the job at home? Start them off with a few suggestions, e.g. *firefighter*, *brain surgeon*, *secretary*, *journalist*, and ask them in each case to justify which category they would put each one into.

1 🔘 **2.37–2.38** Make sure students have read the questions before you play the recording so that they know what information to listen out for. Then play the recording. Students match the items to the speakers. If necessary, play it again for them to check their answers. Elicit students' opinions on what they have heard and whether they were surprised that either job could be done from home.

ANSWERS

a Speaker 2   b Speaker 1   c Speaker 1   d Speaker 2
e Speaker 2   f Speaker 1   g Speaker 2

🔘 **2.37**

1

A: The Internet and other new technologies have changed the way we work and the titles of our jobs. For example, instead of the secretary, meet Jill Spencer, a 'virtual assistant'. Jill, what exactly is a virtual assistant?

B: Virtual assistants, or VAs, work from home. We offer services to businesses which don't have sufficient work to justify employing someone full-time.

A: Why did you decide to be a virtual assistant?

B: I retired from my job as a conference organizer, but I wanted to earn some extra money. I became a VA because it meant I didn't have to leave my country home down here in Cornwall.

A: Yes, it's a lovely place – I can understand why you didn't want to move away. So, how did you start?

B: I had a lot of contacts from my previous work. I began by providing things like bookkeeping, but now I offer a range of services for clients all over the UK.

A: It's going well, then?

B: Yes, I wasn't looking to earn a fantastic amount of money. The biggest advantage is that you can do as little or as much as you want. If it's a lovely sunny day, I can sit out in the garden and do the work in the evening.

A: What do you need to get started?

B: The basic tools are a computer with an Internet connection, a scanner and a mobile phone. Anyone with basic office skills could do the job. Apart from that it depends on the kind of services you're going to offer and what the clients want.

A: And what's in it for the companies?

B: Companies get a huge amount out of it because they only use a virtual assistant when they need one. Also, they can perhaps get someone with a higher professional level than they could get if they had to pay someone full-time. There's also no problem of office hours. A businessman can be out of the office all day, but his assistant is still available in the evening if he needs to discuss things. I think it could make a big difference to everyone's lifestyle.

2.38

2

A: Anna, what exactly do you do?

B: I'm a concierge at the Westin Hotel in Santa Clara, California.

A: What was life like before you became a teleworker?

B: I had to get up at three in the morning so I could shower and dress, take my kids to my mother's, and set off to work by 4.30.

A: 4.30!

B: Yes, there was a lot of traffic. On a good day I got there by 6.30. That gave me half an hour to relax before starting my shift at seven o'clock.

A: It sounds awful.

B: Yes, I was getting up in the dark and getting home in the dark. I never saw my husband or children. I liked my job, but my life was a nightmare.

A: And what is life like now?

B: Oh, I feel like the luckiest person alive. I now get up at 5.30. My mother still looks after the children but I don't have the 80-mile drive to work along Highway 101. We've set up my workplace in one of the bedrooms. I sit down in front of a camera, pin on a microphone and I'm ready for business.

A: How does it work at the hotel?

B: Guests still go up to the concierge desk, but instead of me in person, they see me on a giant TV screen. They can only see my head and shoulders, so I can wear my slippers while I work.

A: What do your employers think about it?

B: Oh, they're happy because they can't afford to lose me. In the hotel industry we don't have the high salaries of Cisco, Palm or Sun Micro, so there's a high turnover of staff. With unemployment around here so low it's hard to replace workers. It cost them $50,000 but they thought it was worth a try.

A: And the guests?

B: They're happy. Apart from anything else they don't have to leave a tip!

2 2.37–2.38 Go through the chart before you play the recording again. With stronger students, you could ask them to complete as much as possible from what they remember from the first listening. Then play the recording. Students can compare their answers with a partner or in small groups before you check answers with the class.

ANSWERS

	Speaker 1	Speaker 2
Country	England (Cornwall)	the USA (Santa Clara, California)
What did she do before?	Conference organizer	Same job (hotel concierge), but not as a teleworker
What does she do now?	Virtual assistant	Hotel concierge (as a teleworker)
What are the advantages of her new work?	She can stay in the country. She can do as much or as little work as she wants. She can work when she chooses.	She doesn't have to get up so early or get home so late. She doesn't have a long drive to work through heavy traffic. She sees more of her husband and children. She can wear her slippers to work if she wants.
What are the advantages for her employers/clients?	They only pay when they need her. They can afford to get someone at a higher professional level. They can use her services outside normal office hours.	They might otherwise have lost her services, and staff are hard to find in the area. The guests seem to be happy to talk to her on a screen, and they don't have to leave a tip.

3 Students discuss the question with a partner. Encourage them to give full reasons for their opinion. Have a class feedback session to compare opinions.

4 Give students plenty of time to read the article. Make sure they understand that they have to identify the correct category for each opinion, and whether it is an advantage or a disadvantage. Allow students to compare answers with a partner or in small groups.

ANSWERS

	Advantages	Disadvantages
Family	4	1
The workplace	13	10
The working day	12	8
Commuting	5	3
Technology	11	15
Efficiency	2	9
Costs	7	6
Motivation	16	14

5 Students check their answers to 4 on page 138.

6 Students will find the vocabulary focused on here useful when they come to talk about work and working situations. Students should scan the article quickly to find the matching words. Then check answers with the class.

ANSWERS

a wind down	b traffic jams	c perks
d workaholics	e gossip	f obsolete
g get down to	h cracking the whip	

7 Students use the words from the previous exercise to complete the sentences. Check the answers by asking students to read out the completed sentences, so that they hear the words in context.

ANSWERS

a gossip	b wind down	c workaholic
d perks	e obsolete	f get down to
g traffic jams	h Cracking the whip	

8 Students discuss with a partner whether or not the sentences in 7 are true for them, and why.

Language links

Direct students to the *Language links* section on page 122, for more on the vocabulary of teleworking.

Stay at home and get rich?

In this section, students look at an Internet advert that promises money for unskilled work at home. They listen to two people discussing the advert, and talk about the advantages and disadvantages of working at home. This leads into some work on conditionals. Students complete sentences from the listening and then complete sentences with information of their own. They then talk about hypothetical changes in their own working conditions.

1 Focus attention on the advert and brainstorm ideas for what the job might entail. Find out how common adverts like this are in students' own language(s) and what sort of jobs they usually involve.

2 2.39 Go through the questions with the class before you play the recording so that they know what information to listen out for. Allow them to make notes while they listen if they wish.

ANSWERS

a No, they don't. They recognize it as a type of pyramid selling, where you have to try to get a lot of other people involved in order to make any money.

b You don't have a long journey to work. It's better for the environment.

c You miss the contact with other people that you get in an office. It's difficult to get anything done if you can't find a quiet place to work. You need self-discipline to get on with the work.

2.39

A: Have you seen this?

B: What?

A: 'Make money while you work at home. No skill required.'

B: Oh, it's not really about working at home. You sign up to a scheme where they say they will pay you to reply to emails or visit pages on the Internet. Then you're supposed to persuade your friends and family to do it.

A: Oh, so it's like pyramid selling.

B: Yes, the more people you get to do it, the more money you make. The idea is to show potential advertisers that they have an audience. I doubt it really works. If it was so easy, everyone would do it.

A: That's a shame. I wouldn't mind working at home if I had the opportunity.

B: I'm not so sure. I wouldn't miss travelling in to work every day, but if I was at home, I'd miss the contact with the people here.

A: That's true, but if you could just come in a couple of days a week, it would be okay. On the other hand, unless you had somewhere quiet to work, it would be difficult to get anything done.

B: Do you think you'd be disciplined enough?

A: I don't know. I would if it was my own business, but otherwise, who knows? It probably sounds more attractive than it would be in reality.

B: They do talk about telework a lot these days. Some people say that if people stopped commuting, it would be much better for the environment.

A: That's probably right but in the end, I think it depends on the type of job you have.

---

3 2.39 Remind students of the work they did on conditionals with *will* in Unit 13. Then do sentence a) with the class as an example. Ask students to identify the verb forms used in the *if* clause (Past Simple) and in the other clause (*would*). Establish that the question is about an imaginary situation in the future. Students then complete the remaining sentences. Go around and check that they are using the forms correctly. Play the recording for them to check their answers.

ANSWERS

a was; would	b wouldn't; had
c was; I'd miss	d could; would be; had; would
e you'd; would; was	f stopped; would

4 Students complete the phrases with their own words. Go around and check that they are forming conditional sentences correctly. Check answers by asking several students to say one of their sentences to the class.

Language links

Direct students to the *Language links* section on page 122 for more on conditionals with future reference (sometimes called Second Conditionals).

5 Students work with a partner to complete the company manager's conditional chain. Check answers by calling on pairs to each read aloud a sentence in the chain. If you have time, ask students to create a chain of their own. You could also have a two-team game in which a member of team A forms a sentence, e.g. *If I won a lot of money, I'd buy a car.* Then a member of team B has to make the next sentence in the chain, e.g. *If I bought a car, I'd drive to Paris next weekend.*, and so on. Teams score a point for each correct sentence. You may want to draw students' attention to the form *If I/he/she/it were …* as an alternative to *If I he/she/it was.* Point out that they are both in common usage, although *If I were …* is viewed by some to be grammatically correct (because it is the correct form of the verb *to be* in the subjunctive voice).

POSSIBLE ANSWER

If I left my job, I'd spend more time at home. If I spent more time at home, I'd be more relaxed. If I were more relaxed, I'd have time to think. If I had time to think, I'd come up with a really great business idea. If I came up with a really great business idea, I'd set up a company. If I set up a company, it would be an enormous success. If it were/was an enormous success, I'd have a lot of responsibilities. If I had a lot of responsibilities, I'd have to work harder than I want to. If I had to work harder than I wanted to, I would be completely stressed out again.

6 Ask students to discuss these questions with a partner, using the conditional structure which they have just practised. Go around and check that they are using the structure correctly. Check answers by asking several students to say their sentences to the class.

Language links

Direct students' attention to the *Language links* section on pages 122–123, where they will find more information on conditionals with future reference, and practice exercises to help them use the structures correctly.

7 This is quite a difficult roleplay, so students will need time to prepare what they are going to say. They may like to do this at home. Remind them that various opinions have been expressed throughout the unit, so they can go back and look for ideas. Allow them to make brief notes, but discourage them from writing a script of what they are going to say. Draw their attention also to the useful vocabulary in the box at the bottom of the exercise and to the *Language links* section on page 122. As students perform their roleplays, go around offering help and encouragement. At the end, find out who 'won' the argument in each pair.

 1:1 Ask your student to prepare one of the roles at home (and to tell you which one he or she has chosen). Prepare your own arguments for the other point of view.

▶ In company interviews Units 17–19
Encourage students to watch the interview and complete the worksheet.

Language links

ANSWERS

Vocabulary
Teleworking
a flexibility b home c office d desk e local f commute

Grammar
Practice 1
a 6 b 1 c 7 d 3 e 4 f 5 g 2

Practice 2
a lived b would take c would get d would go
e would forget f like g would miss h moved i would spend j asked k would let l have m was/were n would go o spent p would see q would have r is s were t will give

Practice 3
a If he worked harder, he'd be more successful.
b If you had enough experience, we would be able to give you the job.
c If he could drive, he wouldn't have to take taxis all the time.
d If I had the information, I would be able to help you.
e If I liked sport, I would go to the gym.
f If he didn't enjoy his job, he wouldn't work long hours.
g If she had a choice, she wouldn't do the job.
h If my car wasn't in the garage, I would be able to take you to the airport.
i If he was more organized, things wouldn't take him a long time.
j If he couldn't afford it, he wouldn't drive an expensive car.

Practice 4
Suggested answers
a If you got up earlier, you wouldn't be late to work so often.
b If you did a computer course, you would find your work easier.
c You would make a better impression if you wore smarter clothes.
d If you had a mobile phone, customers would be able to contact you when you are out of the office.
e You wouldn't be so stressed if you didn't work so hard.
f If you used the Internet, you would be able to find the information you need more quickly.
g You'd do better at the interview if you did some research on the company first.
h If you didn't complain all the time, people would be more sympathetic to your problems.

Practice 5
a What job would you do if you could choose?
b Where would you live if you had to go abroad?
c How would you treat people if you were the boss?
d What language would you learn if you didn't study English?
e How would you earn a living if the salary wasn't important?

Practice 6
a If I told her about it, she'd sack me.
b Unless he gets nervous at the interview, he won't have any problems.
c If I invite Dave, I'll have to invite Sarah, too.
d If I invited Su, I'd have to invite Dave, too
e If you took an aspirin, you'd feel better.
f If I had time, I'd do some gardening.
g Unless he stops driving like a maniac, he'll hurt himself.
h If I knew it, I would give it to you.

20 Working lunch

In this first section, students listen to two businesspeople having a working lunch in Japan. They answer questions and put lines of the conversation in order. They then study some practical expressions for describing different dishes and how they are prepared.

Warm-up

Find out how often students have business lunches, either with colleagues from the same company or business contacts from outside. Ask them to list the kinds of things they talk about over lunch and the kinds of places they take guests for lunch. Elicit any amusing stories or incidents they know which are connected to business lunches.

1 Read the quotation aloud and discuss it with the class. Elicit ideas for other reasons why a business lunch might go wrong and put them on the board. When students have no more ideas, let them turn to page 139 and compare their ideas with those in the article.

2 **2.40** Make sure students have read the situation and the questions before you play the recording so that they know what information to listen out for. Establish that it is most likely that Satomi Tanaka is the host and Neil Klein the guest, as the restaurant is in Japan. Play the recording. Students answer the questions. Then check answers with the class.

ANSWERS

a He likes the décor.
b Satomi does.
c He wants a steak.
d He decides to try unagi (eel).

 2.40

A: This looks like a very nice place, Satomi.
B: Yes, I thought you would like it.
A: Yes, I really like the décor. Er, could you order for both of us, Satomi?

B: Of course. I think we could have some miso soup to start with. They do it very well here.
A: Okay. Sounds good.
B: And then I think you should try some *unagi*.
A: What's that?
B: It's eel – grilled and served on a bed of rice. It's delicious.
A: Hmm, I'm sure it is. Actually, do you think I could have a steak?
B: Well, I'm afraid they don't serve steak here.
A: I'll try the *unagi*, then.
B: Fine. Would you like some sake, or would you prefer some tea?
A: No, no, let's have some sake.
B: Right. Sake it is, then.

3 **2.40** Students work with a partner to number the conversation lines so that they are in the correct order. Encourage them to take one role each and read it aloud to check that it sounds right. Then play the recording again for them to check their answers. Ask students what they do when they are a guest and someone recommends something to eat which they know they will not like or can't eat. Does Neil handle the situation politely?

ANSWER

See listening script above.

---

4 Students work individually to make a list of typical dishes. Then they work with a partner to act out conversations about their dishes. If students come from a variety of countries, encourage them to work with a partner from a different country. This will give more authenticity to their explanations of their local specialities. In monocultural classes, ask students to decide with their partner which dishes foreign visitors are unlikely to have heard of. Then students swap roles and repeat their conversations. Elicit any stories students have about ordering foreign food or entertaining foreign guests.

> **1:1** Make sure you have prepared in advance a list of dishes from your culture which you think your student will not have heard of. Take the role of the host so that your student can practise being the guest, then swap roles.

Down to business

In this section, students learn about the outcome of Neil Klein's business lunch in Japan as he reports back to his boss. They then hear his conversation with Satomi and decide what he did wrong. A short article on doing business in Japan raises issues about the cultural implications of different business attitudes. Students replace the original conversation between Neil and Satomi with one in which he follows the advice in the article. They then discuss their experiences of doing business in different cultures.

Warm-up

Focus attention on the picture at the bottom of the page. Ask students to say what they think is happening (the woman on the right is selling something door to door; the woman on the left is a potential customer who looks a bit suspicious of her visitor). Choose some adjectives to describe both women. Is door-to-door selling common in your students' country / countries? If so, how do they react when someone comes to their door trying to sell something?

1 🔘 **2.41** Make sure students have read the questions before you play the recording, so that they know what information to listen out for. Then play the recording. Ask students to discuss their answers to the questions with a partner or in small groups, then check answers with the class. Ask students to speculate about what went wrong.

ANSWERS

a Although he had a good time, the business trip was not a success.
b Students' own answers, but students might say that Neil's sales technique was too pushy.

🔘 **2.41**

C: So, any news from Tokyo, Neil?

A: No, I'm afraid not, Jeff. It looks like they're not interested.

C: How did it go with Ms Tanaka?

A: Oh, she was really nice. She took me to a great restaurant. Actually, everything went okay until we got down to business.

C: What happened?

A: I don't know. I thought the sale was a sure thing, but she seemed to lose interest. I don't know what I did wrong.

---

2 🔘 **2.42** Play the recording and elicit various ideas on what Neil did wrong.

POSSIBLE ANSWER

Neil's sales technique was too pushy.

🔘 **2.42**

A: Mmm, that was delicious.

B: I'm glad you enjoyed it. So, Neil, tell me about this digital control software. Why do you think we should be interested?

A: Because it's easily the best program for the job on the market.

B: The system we use at the moment works okay. Why should we change?

A: It's a question of costs. It could save you up to 30%. If you look at the competition, there's just no comparison.

B: Can you give me some information about your sales?

A: Er … about two million dollars' worth worldwide.

B: Could I see the documentation?

A: Well, I'm afraid that's confidential, but listen, if we can make a deal today, I can offer you an even better discount.

3 Go through the article with the class and explain anything they don't understand. Ask if the ideas in the article confirm what they thought in 2. If students have experience of doing business in Japan, ask them if their experience matches the advice in the article. If you have Japanese students, ask them if they think the assessment is correct.

4 Students may need time to prepare their conversations and they may find it useful to refer to the listening script on page 158, though they should make notes rather than write out a script for their new conversation. Tell them that they can invent any extra information that they need and draw their attention to the *Useful language* box in the margin of page 125. When they act out their conversations, go around and make a note of any particularly successful conversations which can be performed for the class.

1:1 Ask your student to take the role of Neil, while you play Satomi.

5 This could be done as a class discussion, with students swapping information and experiences.

Meet me halfway

Learning objectives

The issue in this case study is disagreements between colleagues over their working environment, specifically whether they should be allowed to play music at work. Students watch a disagreement between Ralph and Claudia when Ralph objects to the fact that Claudia plays loud music, which he finds distracting. They read an email of complaint to the manager and then see how the parties involved try to negotiate a compromise.

Digital resources: Workplace Scenario E

📹 In company in action E1–E2 and worksheet; extension worksheets; Glossary; Student's Book answer key; Student's Book listening script; Fast-track map; End of course test

Warm-up

Focus attention on the definition of the phrase *meet someone halfway* in the margin. The example sentence here relates to negotiating a business deal, but ask students for ideas of situations that occur between colleagues in an office where both sides need to meet each other halfway in order to solve a disagreement.

1 Students work with a partner to read the article and discuss the questions. Check answers with the class and answer any questions students may have about new vocabulary. Elicit the students' responses to the article and the idea of listening to music at work. Ask them to think of some jobs where music may be helpful, and others where it would not be possible to listen to music and work at the same time.

ANSWERS

a Positive
b They object to members of their team listening to music through headphones at their desks and being cut off from their colleagues.
c Suggested answers: they might not hear the phone ring, leaving other colleagues to answer calls; it might mean that they don't work well as a team if they isolate themselves with headphones; they might be distracted by the music and make mistakes because they are concentrating less on their work.
d We naturally pay attention to words more than sounds, so people might concentrate on listening to the lyrics of a song (even singing along to it) rather than on the work they are supposed to be doing.
e Students' own answers

2 📹 **E1** Go through the questions with the class, then play the video. Students answer the questions. Check answers with the class. Elicit a range of views on d) and have a class vote on whether either of them is right.

ANSWERS

a Claudia is playing music and sometimes singing. Ralph can't concentrate on his work because of it.

b She doesn't like them, and she needs to hear the phone if it rings.
c Ralph says Claudia should respect the fact that he can't work with music in the background. Claudia says Ralph should respect the fact that she can't work without music.
d Students' own answers

📹 **E1**

Ralph: Claudia? Claudia! CLAUDIA!

Claudia: Yes, Ralph?

R: Could you turn it down, please?

C: Pardon?

R: I said, could you turn it DOWN, please?

C: Come on; the song is almost finished and I love this one. Can you wait?

R: NO. I want you to turn it off now!

C: There. Happy?

R: No, not really.

C: What's the problem?

R: I'm trying to work. This is really difficult, and I can't concentrate with loud music playing the whole time.

C: It's not that loud, is it?

R: Yes, it is! And it doesn't help with you singing along.

C: Sorry, I just get a little carried away sometimes. I didn't realize it bothered you that much.

R: Well, it does! Why can't you listen to it on your headphones?

C: I don't like them, and anyway I need to listen for the phone.

R: Well in that case you'll just have to stop playing music.

C: What? Oh come on Ralph, you're being unreasonable. I need music; it helps me to work.

R: Sorry, but I can't concentrate.

C: Meet me halfway on this. I'm happy for you to play your music sometimes.

R: I don't listen to music when I'm working. I don't like it and I can't concentrate.

C: Okay, well why don't I find some nice quiet music? That way, I'll be able to work and you won't be bothered.

R: Look, I don't want to make a fuss, but I really need to get these accounts finished and I can't work with music playing – any kind of music! I need you to respect that.

C: And I can't work WITHOUT music. Why can't YOU respect that?

R: Please, Claudia! I need to get this done and I just want some SILENCE!

C: All right then. I can see you're stressed. I won't play any music.

R: Thank you.

C: Don't mention it.

3 Go through the questions with the class. Students read the email and answer the questions.

ANSWERS

a He wants to discuss the issue of music in the office. He wants either a change in company policy regarding music or a way for both sides to meet halfway.

b Students' own answers

c *I don't want to make a fuss* means *I don't want to cause trouble.*

d Students' own answers

4 Go through the instructions with the class, then students work with a partner and turn to their respective pages. As they perform their roleplays, go around monitoring and assisting where necessary. Make a note of any particularly good roleplays which can be performed for the class.

5 Students individually complete the FEEDBACK: Self-assessment section on page 145 and then discuss their answers with their partner. Ask them if they found anything surprising.

6 **E2** Play the video and ask students to compare Ralph and Claudia's conversation with their own. Then students swap roles and do the roleplay again. Remind them to use as many of the useful phrases from 4 as they can.

▸ E2

Ralph: Morning.

Claudia: Morning. Ralph ...

R: Claudia. Er, Claudia. I'm really sorry ...

C: No really, Ralph, I'm sorry.

R: Wait ... the thing is ... I sent Serena an email yesterday, about the music. I was still angry. I'm really sorry.

C: I know. She spoke to me at the end of the day. It's fine. Really. But, I think we should talk about it.

R: You're right. I mean, you like listening to music whilst working, I don't. But we share the same office, so – as you said yesterday, let's meet halfway. Would you consider a compromise?

C: That would be great. What do you suggest?

R: Well, we could try playing music for part of the day.

C: Okay, so I can listen to music in the morning, but not the afternoon.

R: That would be good. But also, sometimes when I have a deadline coming up, like yesterday, it would be great if I could tell you that and you would know not to play music at all. Just until the deadline. Would that be acceptable?

C: That seems reasonable. Is it okay for me to play music when I've got a deadline? It really helps me to concentrate.

R: Okay, if you give me plenty of warning.

C: Fine.

R: One more thing, I think music with singing is more distracting than instrumental music. Would you consider only playing classical music, or something like that?

C: Really? To be honest, all my favourite music has singing in it. I don't really like classical music.

R: Hmm, I'm not sure what to suggest. Pop songs can be distracting.

C: Would you mind just a little bit of pop music, if I promise never to sing?

R: Okay, it's a deal.

C: Great! So, are you coming out with everyone tonight?

R: Yeah, I think so. Where are we going?

C: Karaoke.

7 Ask students to work in small groups to discuss the questions. Then ask one member of each group to report back to the class on their discussion. Find out what things cause the most disagreement at work.

8 Students work with a partner to have conversations in which they try to meet each other halfway on one of the situations given. Once they have decided on their situation, tell them to spend some time thinking of what opposing viewpoints could be taken, and reasons for those viewpoints. Let them make notes, but discourage them from writing out a full script. As they do their roleplays, go around and make a note of any particularly good ones which can be performed for the class. Alternatively, ask each pair to give a quick summary of their conversation and the way in which they met each other halfway. Encourage discussion of the compromises as a group.

1:1 Let your student choose the situation and the viewpoint they want to take. Make sure you have enough ideas to provide a counter-viewpoint, whatever they choose. Try to hold back so that it is the student who first proposes a solution for meeting you halfway.